HowExpert
to Epoxy Resin Art

101+ Tips to Learn How to Create Epoxy Resin Art for Beginners

HowExpert with Madison Barclay

For more tips related to this topic, visit HowExpert.com/epoxyresinart.

Recommended Resources

- HowExpert.com – How To Guides on All Topics from A to Z by Everyday Experts.
- HowExpert.com/free – Free HowExpert Email Newsletter.
- HowExpert.com/books – HowExpert Books
- HowExpert.com/courses – HowExpert Courses
- HowExpert.com/clothing – HowExpert Clothing
- HowExpert.com/membership – HowExpert Membership Site
- HowExpert.com/affiliates – HowExpert Affiliate Program
- HowExpert.com/jobs – HowExpert Jobs
- HowExpert.com/writers – Write About Your #1 Passion/Knowledge/Expertise & Become a HowExpert Author.
- HowExpert.com/resources – Additional HowExpert Recommended Resources
- YouTube.com/HowExpert – Subscribe to HowExpert YouTube.
- Instagram.com/HowExpert – Follow HowExpert on Instagram.
- Facebook.com/HowExpert – Follow HowExpert on Facebook.
- TikTok.com/@HowExpert – Follow HowExpert on TikTok.

Publisher's Foreword

Dear HowExpert Reader,

HowExpert publishes quick 'how to' guides on all topics from A to Z by everyday experts.

At HowExpert, our mission is to discover, empower, and maximize everyday people's talents to ultimately make a positive impact in the world for all topics from A to Z...one everyday expert at a time!

All of our HowExpert guides are written by everyday people just like you and me, who have a passion, knowledge, and expertise for a specific topic.

We take great pride in selecting everyday experts who have a passion, real-life experience in a topic, and excellent writing skills to teach you about the topic you are also passionate about and eager to learn.

We hope you get a lot of value from our HowExpert guides, and it can make a positive impact on your life in some way. All of our readers, including you, help us continue living our mission of positively impacting the world for all spheres of influences from A to Z.

If you enjoyed one of our HowExpert guides, then please take a moment to send us your feedback from wherever you got this book.

Thank you, and we wish you all the best in all aspects of life.

Sincerely,

Byungjoon "BJ" Min / 민병준
Founder & Publisher of HowExpert
HowExpert.com

PS...If you are also interested in becoming a HowExpert author, then please visit our website at HowExpert.com/writers. Thank you & again, all the best! John 3:16

Table of Contents

Introduction

In the enchanting world of art, epoxy resin has emerged as a transformative medium that allows artists to craft intricate, vibrant, and captivating pieces. Epoxy resin art is a unique form of artwork that involves the use of epoxy resins to create aesthetically pleasing pieces. When combined with pigment, beads, glitters, and other materials, it can be used to produce stunning, multidimensional creations. Epoxy resin art is a mesmerizing form of artwork that can bring any space to life. With the right materials and techniques, epoxy resin can be used to create a wide range of stunning visual effects.

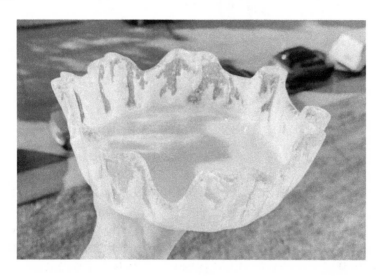

These are both beautiful creations made with epoxy resin.

Whether you want to adorn your walls with a colorful landscape, craft intricate jewelry designs, or make a one-of-a-kind sculpture, epoxy resin art provides endless possibilities for creative expression.

Epoxy resin art has grown exponentially over recent years; it has become an increasingly popular form of creative expression, allowing artists to explore new realms of possibilities with each piece they create. Epoxy resin art isn't limited to one type of artwork; artists have found ways to incorporate this medium into landscapes, abstract paintings, sculptures, jewelry making, woodworking projects, and more! This versatility has made epoxy resin one of the most sought-after forms of art in the world.

Whether you're an aspiring artist or a seasoned creator, this book will serve as your comprehensive guide to mastering the art of working with epoxy resin. From understanding the fundamentals of epoxy resin to mastering techniques, you will be taken on a journey through the mesmerizing realm of resin art. With each turn of the page, you'll uncover valuable insights, tips, and tricks that will empower you to create stunning art pieces that reflect your unique vision.

Think of this book as your gateway to unlocking the secrets of epoxy resin art. As you explore this unique medium, you'll find yourself captivated by its vibrant colors and mesmerizing textures. Epoxy resin art is sure to leave a lasting impression on everyone who lays eyes upon your masterpieces! So, let's begin this exploration together, and may your creativity flow as beautifully as the resin you work with.

Chapter 1: What is Epoxy Resin?

Epoxy Resin

Before delving into the world of epoxy resin art, it is essential to gain a comprehensive understanding of epoxy resin's properties and characteristics. This intricate process of creating using epoxy resin requires the mixture of two liquid substances, which seamlessly unite to form a solid, mesmerizing piece, captivating the attention of all. As one explores the magical process of creating with epoxy resin, one will undoubtedly become as entranced by its allure as I was.

When I first started using epoxy resin, I was clueless about the process and its properties. I didn't take any precautions to protect myself, my workspace, or my clothes from potential spills. While working with the material, I was unaware of the fumes that epoxy resin releases into the air. I didn't even know epoxy resin was a chemical. My knowledge about epoxy resin was limited to information from posts in social media groups and videos showcasing quick, 30-second clips of people pouring liquid into silicone molds and later presenting a glass-like object. Basically, I would see people pouring colorful liquid and have these fantastic results. The simplicity of the craft piqued my interest, and I wanted to try it myself. However, before taking the plunge and ordering my own epoxy resin, I watched more videos and read about the craft in more online groups for six months. Looking back, I realize that even with my research, I had no actual knowledge of the chemical properties of epoxy resin, and I only thought of it as an exciting and new creative medium.

My first attempt at using epoxy resin was a complete disaster. I had set out to create a beautiful moon-shaped shelf with a white base, dried leaves, and stunning gold foils. However, I made the grave mistake of not taking the necessary precautions or adequately preparing myself for the task at hand. In my haste, I worked on my wooden dining room floor, clad only in shorts and a sports bra, leaving my skin and the floor exposed to the potent and hazardous adhesive. Adding insult to injury, I even went ahead and touched the chemicals directly with my bare hands and allowed my long hair to flow freely around me.

I soon realized that I had made some serious mistakes. Due to my lack of experience and preparation, I developed a painful chemical rash on my skin. In addition, my hardwood floors were irreparably damaged. To top it off, even the finished epoxy resin piece I had worked on had pieces of my hair stuck in it. Despite these setbacks, I was still drawn to the craft. In fact, I quickly became addicted to it, especially after creating a stunning shelf (minus the hair).

This is a photo of my first resin piece, the moon, and star shelf.

Tip #1: Learn before you start.

As a result of my first experience with epoxy resin, I learned how important it was to take safety measures and be prepared before trying anything new. It was a good reminder that we should never forget about safety when dealing with potentially harmful substances. My rash lasted for over a month and covered my whole body. It was not an enjoyable time. With no limitations on usage, learning how to work with epoxy resin can unlock endless artistic possibilities and potential when used with the proper protective gear.

Tip #2: Remember to prioritize safety in everything you do.

To simplify the term "epoxy resin," it is vital to break the words down into their basic components. Epoxy resin is an adhesive material that comprises polymers of epoxides.

It's kind of like a sort of glue. In liquid form, any epoxy adhesive is considered epoxy resin. Epoxy resin consists of two primary agents or parts: part A, the *hardener* (curing component), and part B, the *resin*. When these two parts are mixed, a chemical reaction occurs, which causes the formation of a hardened or cured piece. This reaction is known as *the curing process*, whereby the combination of the agents produces heat, which transforms the liquid form into a solid form.

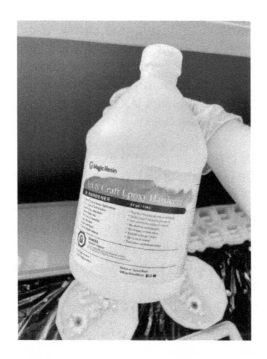

This is an example of a bottle of Part A: hardener.

This is an example of a bottle of Part B: resin.

Epoxy resin is a valuable adhesive that can be used for numerous different purposes. Although its most common use is for coating countertops and floors, this medium can be used for creating furniture, sealing paintings, making jewelry, and creating both 3D and flat art. Epoxy resin is also a potent bonding agent that can bond to various surfaces such as wood, fabric, glass, or metal.

Although different types of resin are available, each with its unique curing process, the benefits of using epoxy resin are undeniable. The cured product is exceptionally durable, waterproof, and resistant to wear, cracking, and peeling, making it easy to maintain quality. Furthermore, quality epoxy resin does not yellow over time and retains its shape, regardless of the application. With the proper molding, epoxy resin can form any shape desired. When it is managed with care and precision, epoxy resin has the ability to work wonders as a medium.

Types & Categories of Epoxy Resin

The Different Categories

Epoxy resin can be broadly classified into two categories: coating resin and casting resin. Coating resin is particularly suited to creating a glossy and transparent surface finish, while casting resin mainly produces solid pieces that resemble plastic. Ultimately, the decision to use either coating or casting resin will depend on the project's specific requirements, such as the intended function and desired appearance.

Coating resins are typically utilized to give materials such as metal or wood a more durable, moisture-resistant, glossy finish. Coating resin generally is denser than casting resin, resulting in a longer curing time. Once cured, coating resin is tougher and more long-lasting than casting resin, making it an ideal option for coating projects that require scratch resistance. If you're looking to use molds or create intricate details with resin, casting resin is the ideal choice. Compared to coating resin, casting resin has a thinner consistency.

The Different Types

There are several types of epoxy resin that each have their own distinctive attributes and benefits. All resin types fall into either the category of casting resin or coating resin. This guidebook focuses on the four types commonly used for art projects: tabletop resin, arts and crafts resin, deep pour/casting resin, and UV resin.

Tip #3: Choose quality over price when picking epoxy resin.

Tabletop resin, arts and crafts resin, and deep pour/casting resin are all casting resins and share a few similarities, such as the need for a hardener and resin to initiate the curing process. However, there are significant differences between these types of resin that are worth noting. For instance, the amount of mixed epoxy resin that can be poured into a single vessel varies depending on the specific epoxy resin used. Additionally, the working time for each of these types of resin is different. Therefore, it's essential to understand the differences between these types of resin to choose the right one for your project.

If you aim to produce intricate, multi-layered projects, cover paintings, use shallow molds, or seal large art pieces (such as tables), you have two excellent options: tabletop resin and arts and crafts resin. It's important to note that tabletop resin can generally be poured up to a maximum depth of ¼ inch, whereas arts and crafts resin can generally be poured up to a depth of ½ inch at a time. Choosing the appropriate type of resin based on your project's requirements and specifications is important in order to achieve the best possible results.

If you require a substantial amount of resin to fill a deep space ranging from 2 to 4 inches in depth, it is recommended that you opt for deep pour/casting resin. This resin type is specifically designed to meet your needs and provides a reliable and durable solution for your project.

It is crucial to avoid overpouring when working with resin as it can generate excessive heat during the curing process, which can lead to unfavorable results or damaged pieces.

Tip #4: Use water as a measuring tool.

Measure how much resin you will need before you start by using water to avoid overpouring.

"*Working time*" is a vital factor to consider when working with resin as an artist. This term refers to the duration in which the resin remains in its liquid state and can be manipulated before it begins to cure. It is essential to note that the working time may vary depending on the type of resin used. For instance, tabletop and arts and crafts resin typically offer a 30-minute window to work with the mixture once all agents have been combined. However, the working time for deep pour/casting resin is typically longer and may range from 3 to 6 hours. Therefore, it is essential to consider the type of project you are working on and select the appropriate resin with a working time that suits your needs.

Tip #5: Make every second of your working time count.

UV resin is entirely different from the types of resin previously discussed. UV resin is a coating resin that does not require two agents to be mixed. It comes as one ready-to-go liquid. To activate the curing process for this type of resin, all one needs to do is expose it to UV light (typically done with a UV lamp). One drawback of using this particular resin is its limited pouring capacity of up to 4mm.

UV resin typically has a shelf life of around six months and has the longest working time compared to other epoxy resins since no hardening agent is involved. UV resin also cures the fastest and requires minimal heat to harden. Unlike other epoxy resins that take days to solidify, UV resin can harden in just a few minutes when exposed to UV light or sunlight. When looking for a UV lamp compatible with UV resin, the UV strength should be a minimum of 4 watts.

The straightforward nature of UV resin makes it suitable for creating smaller-scale crafts, such as jewelry or bookmarks. Additionally, it is frequently used as a protective coating or gloss for larger projects.

This is an example of a stunning pair of earrings made with UV resin.

The Science Behind the Art

Did you know epoxy resin belongs to a class of polymer compounds contained in epoxide groups? I certainly did not.

Enhancing your knowledge about the chemical processes involved in resin work can greatly improve your resin skills.

Epoxy resin is made by combining two different components, namely the hardener and the resin, which form a powerful chemical bond when mixed together. In the case of UV resin, the resin and UV light are the two different components. Additionally, epoxy resin also contains hydroxyl groups that allow it to adhere to various surfaces and materials.

One crucial thing to remember is the chemical reaction that occurs during the curing process generates heat. This heat causes the epoxy resin's surface to change from a liquid state to a solid form. It is essential to note that the resin and hardener should be mixed without any other additives, and any additional materials should only be added during the artist's working time. In other words, when adding color to your resin, wait until both parts are mixed thoroughly.

It is highly recommended to double-check the instructions for your specific epoxy resin brand before mixing the resin and hardener together. This is because each brand may differ in properties, and you want to ensure that you achieve the best possible results for your project. Following these guidelines, you can create beautiful and long-lasting works of art with epoxy resin.

Tip #6: Always double-check your resin's instructions.

Creating Art with Resin

Epoxy resin can be used in many ways, but the most imaginative application is undoubtedly in the realm of art. Using epoxy resin to create art pieces one can cherish for life gives an indescribable feeling. Art is a unique concept in that the perception of art pieces can change with each viewer, and art can hold many different meanings or emotions depending on the individual observer. What one may find hideous, the other could find life-changingly beautiful. Visual effects can play a vital role in the impact of art, and epoxy resin is a flexible medium that enables the creation of functional art pieces, three-dimensional sculptures, and wall art, among other endless possibilities.

Tip #7: Never limit your imagination.

Functional art can be defined as artistic objects that serve a function. I have always played around in different creative fields, and when I first started to think about using resin, the idea of art serving a purpose was what captivated me the most. I loved the concept of art hidden within everyday objects.

This serving bowl is an example of functional art created with epoxy resin.

Have you ever envisioned a collection of coasters that resemble the captivating sight of waves crashing onto the shore?

These beautiful coasters would not only add a touch of elegance to any living space, but they would also serve a functional purpose by protecting your furniture from unappealing beverage stains. Coasters are such a fun way for people to incorporate art into their everyday lives. I find it delightful to imagine someone starting their day by brewing a cup of coffee, taking it outside, and resting it on one of the beautiful coasters I've designed.

Or perhaps you would be intrigued by this - a resin cone sculpture embellished with delicate dried flowers and shimmering gold foils, presented against a crystal-clear backdrop. It not only serves as a charming, decorative piece for your home but also serves as a functional and aesthetically pleasing storage solution for your rings.

As a newlywed, I often searched for a safe spot to keep my rings while crafting. These lovely floral designs turned out to be the ideal solution for me.

Tip #8: Find art in the unexpected.

Just because art can be functional doesn't mean it always has to be. Still, functional art opens endless doors of possibility. As an artist, I also love to create floral statues. These three-dimensional statues are shaped like a female body and have a transparent background filled with dried flowers. I have silicone molds that make various female forms ranging in sizes of all kinds, giving me all the freedom I need to create beautiful statues. An artist can create many three-dimensional objects like figurines, sculptures, statues, and paperweights with epoxy resin.

This is a floral statue created with epoxy resin.

Often three-dimensional silicone molds are used to easily preserve special objects. For example, many artists use three-dimensional silicone pyramid molds to encase their wedding florals. The result is a stunning home decoration that showcases sentimental and long-lasting blooms. Using resin and three-dimensional molds allows artists to explore their creative potential and produce unique and meaningful artwork.

Did you know that epoxy resin can be used for wall art in three different ways?

Firstly, it can be used to seal and protect any painting, providing a glossy, water-resistant, and durable finish. Alternatively, it can be used to create abstract paintings by pouring different colored resins onto a canvas to produce a beautiful, marbled effect. Lastly, you can also use flat silicone molds to make beautiful and creative wall hangings.

This is an example of a wall hanging made using epoxy resin.

Have you ever thought of personalizing your furniture or creating a fashionable river table? Look no further than epoxy resin - the ideal solution for your needs.

Although silicone molds are widely used, there are various other options available, such as using wooden, plastic, or metal bases. You can even employ modeling clay to craft an intricately designed border, pour the resin onto a plastic base, and allow it to solidify into a stunning piece that can be used as a tray or wall art. With epoxy resin, the possibilities are endless!

This tray was made by pouring resin on a metal surface, resulting in a stunning and smooth finish.

Chapter Summary

Let's take a moment to go over what we've covered in this chapter to make sure you have a good understanding of all the important concepts.

By reading this chapter, you have learned about the following:

- what exactly epoxy resin consists of & the properties behind the medium
- the different categories & types of epoxy resin
- how to select the resin to work with
- how the hardening of liquid resin begins through a chemical reaction
- different ways to use or create with the medium

Having finished this chapter, you should have a solid grasp of these key terms:

1. working time
2. curing process
3. resin
4. hardener

Now that you have a solid grasp of the medium, it's time to move on to the next phase of working with epoxy resin: setting up your workspace.

Chapter 2: Setting Up Your Workspace

Setting up your artistic workspace can be a fun task but one that must be thought through. I have made the mistake of rushing into a project without setting up everything I needed beforehand, and the results of my project were far from what I wanted to accomplish. Once I gained more experience using epoxy resin, I knew setting up my workspace was crucial for creating my masterpieces. Through research and practice, I determined that three areas need special attention before I begin any epoxy resin project: equipment, space, and protection.

Tip #9: Always take the time to think before you start.

First, I needed a well-ventilated area to work in, as the fumes from the epoxy resin can be toxic. I set up a small fan to circulate the air and opened the windows to let in fresh air. I also needed a level surface to work on, so I set up a sturdy table in my apartment. I lined the surface with plastic sheets (or garbage bags) to protect it from any spills or drips. Next, I made sure to wear protective gear, such as gloves, safety glasses, and a mask, to prevent any contact with the resin or inhalation of the fumes.

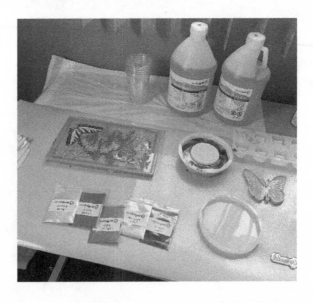

This is an example of a prepared workstation.

Tip #10: Keep a fan running to help disperse the fumes released during the curing process.

In addition, I gathered all the necessary tools, such as measuring cups, mixing sticks, and a heat gun. I made sure to have enough epoxy resin on hand for my project and pigments, glitter, and other materials to add to the resin for a unique touch.

Tip #11: Avoid moisture.

Keep your workspace dry to prevent unwanted bubbles or cloudiness in your resin.

With my workspace set up correctly and protective gear in place, I continued my work confidently and excitedly, knowing that I had taken all the necessary steps to ensure my safety and create a masterpiece. Let's teach you what you need to know.

Equipment Requirements

Here's a list of essential items you'll need:

1. Epoxy Resin: Choose a high-quality epoxy resin suitable for your project. Check the mixing ratios and curing times provided by the manufacturer.

2. Hardener: This is the catalyst that initiates the curing process when mixed with epoxy resin. Always use the recommended hardener for the resin you've chosen.

3. Mixing Cups: Plastic or silicone cups are recommended. Plastic cups can be used for quick and easy disposable cleanup, while silicone cups can be cleaned and reused. I recommend always using cups with measuring lines on them to ensure proper mixing ratios.

I like having different sized plastic cups on hand.

Tip #12: Plastic cups with ridges make for easier measuring.

4. Stir Sticks: Wooden or plastic stir sticks are essential for mixing resin and hardener together thoroughly. Avoid using metal, as it could cause unwanted reactions. I often use popsicle sticks or plastic cutlery.

I often use plastic knives for stir sticks.

Tip #13: When using plastic cutlery as stir sticks, always use the neck. Using the proper end often causes more bubbles when stirring.

5. Safety Gear: Wear nitrile gloves to protect your hands from direct contact with epoxy resin. Safety glasses or goggles will shield your eyes from potential splashes. Make sure all your skin is covered and you aren't emotionally attached to the clothing you are wearing.

Tip #14: For extra protection, invest in a plastic protection suit to cover your clothing.

6. Ventilation: If your workspace lacks good ventilation, consider using a respirator mask with organic vapor cartridges to prevent inhaling harmful fumes.

Tip #15: Work outside, if you can, to avoid having to worry about fumes.

7. Heat Gun, Lighter, or Torch: These tools help eliminate bubbles from your resin once poured onto your artwork.

Tip #16: Lighters are a great budget-friendly option for smaller areas and molds.

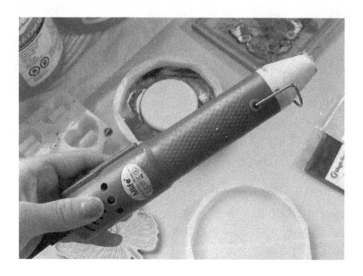

This is an example of a heat gun used with epoxy resin.

Tip #17: Make sure you never bring your heat gun too close to your silicone molds.

This will damage your molds and affect their longevity.

8. Table Cover: Covering your workspace with something to protect your table is essential. I recommend using plastic or silicone. My go-to is a large black garbage bag, which lays flat, holds molds in place, and the hardened resin peels off.

During this resin session, a white plastic garbage bag is used as a table cover.

We have discussed the essential items for the job, yet there are other materials and tools that could prove to be helpful. Here's a short list of extra options for you to consider.

1. Silicone Mat or Non-Stick Craft Sheet: These provide a clean and easy-to-clean surface to work on, preventing resin from sticking to your workspace.

2. Resin Leveling Tools: Tools like resin spreaders or palette knives can help you evenly spread and distribute resin across your artwork's surface.

Tip #18: Silicone spatulas are a great resin spreader that leaves the resin smooth.

3. Resin Calculator: Especially useful when working on larger projects, a resin calculator helps you determine the correct amount of resin and hardener to mix, reducing wastage.

Tip #19: If you're creating resin jewelry, having a selection of jewelry findings like bezels, chains, earring hooks, and jump rings can help you finish your pieces professionally.

4. Resin Dispensing Bottles: These bottles make it easier to measure and pour the precise amounts of resin and hardener needed for your project, reducing the risk of mistakes.

5. Paint Brushes: Small, fine-tipped brushes can be used to apply resin to intricate areas or add details to your artwork.

6. Pipettes and Droppers: These are useful for precise color mixing, adding pigments, dyes, or other liquids to your resin mixture.

7. Masking Tape or Painter's Tape: These can be used to create clean lines and protect specific areas of your artwork while working with resin.

8. Fine Sandpaper or Polishing Pads: These tools can help you smooth out imperfections on the resin surface and achieve a high-gloss finish.

9. Resin Sealant Spray: A clear sealant spray can add an extra layer of protection to your cured resin artwork, safeguarding it from UV light and preventing yellowing over time.

Tip #20: Sealant sprays are great for 3D pieces as they provide great, full, and even coverage.

Space Requirements

Creating a suitable workspace is essential for successfully completing your epoxy resin art projects. Make sure you give yourself plenty of room to spread out all the supplies and materials you will need for each project.

To begin, select a flat and level surface to prevent imperfections in the resin. Ideally, this would be some sort of large workbench or table in an open space with plenty of ventilation.

Tip #21: If you don't have access to a table, work on your floor!

Cover the workspace with a plastic mat or other material that can be cleaned easily and will not absorb the resin. This way, bits of resin that drip or splatter will not cause damage or leave unsightly stains behind. Secondly, turn on the lights and clean up any messes before starting your project so you don't get distracted by cleaning while you're working on your jewelry. A tidy workspace is also more appealing than one covered in tools and scraps. Finally, have all of your supplies and tools handy, and gather all the necessary materials beforehand so you don't spend time running around looking for something as you're trying to make a gorgeous piece of art.

Personal Protection Requirements

As I am sure we all know by now, when I started working with epoxy resin, I was completely in the dark. As detailed in Chapter One, my first experience with this material resulted in a particularly severe chemical reaction. Initially, it manifested as an extremely itchy rash on my arms which quickly spread throughout my legs. In my confusion and distress, I was unable to identify the source of the symptoms. It took me two long weeks before I made the link between my rash and my work with resin.

Looking back on it now, I feel very fortunate that things did not turn out much worse.

After five weeks of suffering, the rash faded away - although had I not taken proper precautions, I could have had permanent damage inflicted upon me. Through further research, I uncovered exactly how dangerous contact with epoxy resin can be; not only is direct skin contact hazardous, but even exposure to its toxic fumes emitted during the curing process can be lethal to both humans and animals.

Tip #22: Safety comes first when working with resin.

To protect yourself, you will need to follow these precautions:

1. Put on some gloves: Nitrile gloves are ideal for protecting your hands from the compounds in epoxy resin. Not only will they shield your skin from contamination, but they also come in handy when handling liquids and solvents as well or cleaning up any messes that get made.

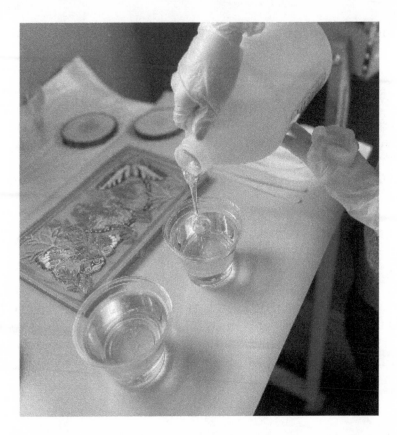

Note here how the artist pouring resin is wearing gloves for protection.

2. Protect your eyes: Safety glasses are a must-have item for resin production. They can help prevent splashes from getting into your eyes and causing irritation, which could lead to pain in the long run.

3. Dress appropriately: When working with epoxy resin, you want to make sure you're wearing proper clothing that accommodates the use of disposable nitrile gloves. Long sleeves and pants will minimize contact with harmful compounds while still allowing for comfort during extended work sessions.

Tip #23: If you don't have old clothes available, avoid getting stains on what you wear now by covering up everything but your face and hands. This includes wrists, arms, and legs.

4. Respiratory protection: In case your workspace isn't correctly ventilated, use a respirator mask with organic vapor cartridges to prevent you from breathing in hazardous fumes. Respirator masks are lightweight and easy to clean, so they won't impede your job performance while protecting against most chemicals encountered in resin production.

Chapter Summary

Let's take a moment to go over what we've covered in this chapter to make sure you have a good understanding of the three areas that need special attention when starting your resin journey.

By reading this chapter, you will have learned about:

- the importance of setting up your workspace
- the different basic equipment you will need to start
- additional equipment that can be helpful
- how you can protect yourself against the chemical
- how you can protect your space from damage

Having finished this chapter, you should have a solid grasp of these key terms:

1. safety gear
2. ventilation
3. workspace
4. hardener

Chapter 3: Getting Started

Now that you have learned about the material and how to set up your workspace, it is time to get started!

Here an artist is playing with her placement of a paper butterfly before she starts her resin project.

Plan Out Your Piece

When starting any creative endeavor, it is essential to have a plan of attack. This is especially true of resin art, where the layout of your piece can make or break it. When starting out your resin art piece, you must go through what steps you are going to take. Is the piece going to be one color? Will it have layers and add-ins? Which layers have to go first? What do you want the final piece to look like? If you don't have a plan or your materials ready in a timely manner, it could result in you having to alter your design.

Tip #24: Plan inclusions. Arrange your inclusions in the mold before pouring resin to ensure they're placed exactly where you want them.

You never want to approach a project blindly. For example, to craft a beautiful black resin tray with white dried flowers, you must begin by making sure all of your materials are prepared. Start mixing your resin slowly. Ensure that you are scraping the sides of your mixing cup and getting your stir stick all the way to the bottom.

Here you can see a resin artist scraping the sides of their cup to get every last drop of resin.

Tip #25: Figure eights and circular stirring help the resin mix better.

Once your resin is mixed, you would then want to pour a layer of clear resin and leave it to sit overnight to give your piece a clearer, shinier finish. This is not needed, but it does enhance your finished result. The next layer is going to be what you want to see on the face of the piece. In this example, that would be white dried flowers. You would pour an even layer of resin and place in your flowers. If their positions need adjusting, you could use your stir stick to gently move them. Leave the piece to set.

When ready, it's time to move on to the next layer. Make sure, when pouring every layer into your mold or over any shape, that it evenly covers all areas so that each section is coated in resin. Take your time and be patient with each layer, as it could make all the difference in the final result. For this final layer, you would take your mixed clear resin and add in whatever colorant you are choosing to use. Do this by adding it to your mixed resin and stirring slowly until the coloring is mixed all the way to the bottom. If the color isn't mixed in correctly, your piece will end up blotchy.

Tip #26: To create an even, black hue – use acrylic paint as your colorant.

Pour the black resin into your mold on top of the flowers. Fill the mold to the very top and pop any bubbles that arise with your heat gun. This is when it would be time to walk away and leave your piece to cure fully. Always check your resin's instructions to find out the full curing time, but I recommend leaving your piece to cure, without touching it, for at least 48 hours.

Tip #27: Take your time with each layer, ensuring that it is properly mixed and poured in order to achieve a professional finish.

It is essential to plan ahead when designing something like this, as the order of the layers plays a big role in how an object turns out. If you added the black resin in the last layer, the flowers wouldn't be visible.

Tip #28: If creating a more complex piece that uses more layers or add-ins, make your layers thinner to allow for more design to show.

I understand that it isn't always necessary to plan ahead, and your creative process is totally valid. However, when you first start using this medium, it's important to keep track of what you're doing.

This is an example for a black resin tray with white dried flowers.

It's not always easy for me to come up with something to make, and I know I am not the only one who struggles with that. When I hit a creative wall, it can take a while to decide on a project. To get started, I often pick out a few colors and think of ways to combine them. Otherwise, I'll look at the supplies I have available and see what sparks my imagination. If I only have a rough outline but don't know where to start, sketching it out or writing down what I'm thinking of doing can help clarify the idea.

Tip #29: To find inspiration, lay your material out in front of you.

Having all your supplies in front of you makes it easier for your brain to come up with an idea.

Gather Your Supplies

Once you have a solid plan in place, it is time to gather your supplies. This includes all of the equipment you will need, as well as the materials and personal protection gear you will be using.

When gathering supplies for an epoxy resin project, start with the basics. First, you'll need your chosen epoxy resin, which is available in different sizes and grades depending on the specific project. Then you will need mixing cups and sticks to blend the epoxy together. You will also need a heat gun or some sort of heat for popping any air bubbles that occur during mixing and pouring.

Tip #30: Measure how much resin you will need to mix by filling your mold with water.

Pour out the water into a measuring cup, and voila! You have the amount needed.

You will also need to collect materials that are suitable for casting or molding into your project. This can include wood, metal, stone, glass fibers, shells, and other items, depending on your particular project. It's important to select materials that can withstand the curing temperatures required by your chosen epoxy formula when creating molds and casts.

Tip #31: Collect enough material so that you have plenty of options while working on your design.

To protect yourself from the hazardous fumes and chemicals involved in working with epoxy resin, you must also collect the proper safety gear. This includes approved respirators to prevent inhalation of toxic vapors, gloves, and protective eyewear when handling the materials or pouring the epoxy. Make sure you have a well-ventilated workspace so that these chemical fumes can be safely released without any harm to yourself or others.

When gathering all of your supplies for your project, be mindful of any specific instructions recommended by your epoxy manufacturer, as some formulas may require special tools, materials, or techniques in order to work effectively. Doing research before starting will ensure that you have everything necessary for a successful project outcome.

Now that you've gathered all of your supplies, it is time to start building! With patience and creativity, your project will come together according to plan and create something beautiful that you can enjoy for years to come.

Ready, Set, Go!

Once you have gone through the planning process and have all your materials gathered, the next stage is to get started and mix your resin. Depending on whether or not you are using two-part resin, it cannot be stressed enough to make sure that you read the instructions thoroughly and adhere to any safety warnings. Once your resin is mixed

together, it is time to start pouring! If your piece has multiple layers, begin with the first layer and strive for a thin layer so that it sets quickly and evenly. Place something beneath your project to catch any messy drips that may occur.

*You can see here the artist has already dripped her resin.
Thankfully there is a silicone mat to protect her table.*

When your mold is filled, you can now set your piece aside for a few hours or overnight in order to let the piece harden completely. The object should be clear of bubbles and look somewhat shiny when set.

Tip #32: When checking if your resin has set properly, give it a gentle tap with something like a wooden spoon or popsicle stick.

Here, the artist is tapping her piece to see if her layer has set.

Once all of your layers have been poured and left to set, it's time to remove your piece from the mold. This can be tricky, so make sure to follow the mold instructions carefully. If you are having difficulty getting the piece out, try placing it in the freezer for a few minutes to loosen it up.

Tip #33: If the mold is 3D, try adding a little soap and water to get your finished piece out.

Finally, take a step back and admire your hard work. Resin art can be a challenging but rewarding process, so don't be afraid to experiment with different techniques and designs. Who knows, you may create a masterpiece that you never thought possible.

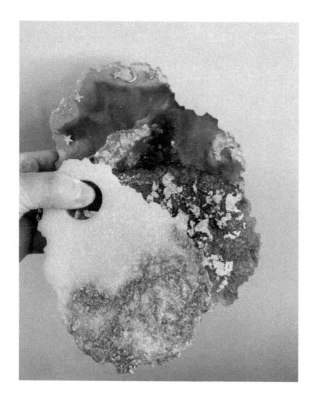

Here are some examples of finished resin pieces. These are miniature paint palettes.

Chapter Summary

Let's take a moment to go over what we've covered in this chapter to make sure you have a good understanding of how to get started.

By reading this chapter, you have learned about the following:

- the importance of creating a plan
- what exactly is important to prepare
- which supplies you need to have gathered
- the basic steps of creating a resin piece
- how to get over creative roadblocks when planning

Chapter 4: Mixing Resin

Mixing Ratios

Mixing epoxy resin can be tricky, but with the proper ratios, you'll achieve great results. Epoxy resin typically consists of two components: the resin itself and the hardener. The mixing ratio is crucial for proper curing and the strength of the final product. When working with two-part epoxy resin, the mixing ratio refers to the proportion of the resin and hardener that must be combined to achieve proper curing. This ratio is crucial for the resin to set correctly and achieve the desired properties.

Tip #34: Common mixing ratios are 1:1, 2:1, or 3:1. This indicates the volume or weight of resin to hardener.

For example, a 2:1 mixing ratio means you would mix two parts of resin with one part of hardener. It's essential to measure the components accurately to ensure a proper chemical reaction. Inaccurate ratios might result in incomplete curing, weak bonds, or other undesirable effects.

This is an example of a 1:1 ratio. Displayed is equal parts epoxy resin and hardener.

Accurate measurement is crucial when working with epoxy resin. Use graduated mixing cups, scales, or syringes designed for epoxy to ensure precise measurement of the resin and hardener. Even a slight deviation from the recommended ratio can affect the resin's performance. Maintaining a consistent mixing ratio is essential for achieving consistent results. Using different mixing ratios can lead to varying levels of hardness, clarity, and curing times in the final product.

Always follow the manufacturer's instructions for the specific epoxy resin you're using, as mixing ratios can vary between different brands and types of epoxy. Additionally, make sure to mix the resin and hardener thoroughly, usually for a specified amount of time, to ensure even distribution and proper curing.

Tip #35: Prior to mixing the resin and hardener, it's a good practice to gently warm the containers in a warm water bath to reduce the viscosity and make mixing easier.

Mixing Times

Mixing epoxy resin for the right amount of time is crucial for achieving proper curing and a successful end result.

Always start by carefully reading the manufacturer's instructions on the epoxy resin packaging, as different brands and types of epoxy resin may require specific mixing times. Generally, you'll want to mix epoxy resin until evenly distributed to avoid sticky spots and ensure consistent curing. Stir gently, avoiding vigorous movements that might introduce air bubbles into the mixture. Use a spatula or stirring stick to scrape the sides and bottom of the container to incorporate any unmixed resin and hardener. Mix until you get a uniform color and texture, with the epoxy appearing clear and free from streaks or swirls of either the resin or the hardener. Don't rush the process but also avoid overmixing, as this can generate excessive heat due to an exothermic reaction and shorten pot life.

Tip #36: To keep track of time, set a timer when you begin mixing.

This will help you achieve proper consistency without going over.

Remember that the specific mixing times can vary based on the epoxy resin brand and type, as well as environmental factors like temperature. Always refer to the instructions provided by the manufacturer, and don't hesitate to reach out to them if you have any questions about mixing times.

Working Times

The "working time" of epoxy resin, also known as the "open time," refers to the period during which the epoxy mixture remains fluid and workable after it has been mixed. Beginners need to be aware of this timeframe to ensure that they have enough time to apply the epoxy, remove air bubbles, and achieve their desired results.

Tip #37: Calculate how much time you'll need for each step of your project, from mixing to application.

This will help you allocate your working time wisely and avoid any last-minute rushes.

Working time is an essential consideration when using epoxy resin. By planning ahead, staying calm, and practicing, you'll be able to make the most of the time you have to create beautiful epoxy projects.

Tip #38: Keep in mind that temperature can influence working time.

Higher temperatures can accelerate the curing process, reducing your working time. Conversely, cooler temperatures might extend it.

Epoxy resin has a limited "pot life," which is the time you have to work with it before it starts to thicken and cure. This can vary based on the brand and specific product, so be sure to check the instructions. It's best to mix only as much resin as you can use within the given pot life. This is a critical factor to consider when working with epoxy because once the pot life expires, the resin will start to cure and harden, making it difficult to apply smoothly or make any changes to your project.

Here are some important points to understand about pot life:

1. Duration: Pot life varies from product to product and can range from a few minutes to several hours. Always refer to the manufacturer's instructions on the product packaging or their official documentation to know the specific pot life for the epoxy resin you are using.

2. Temperature Dependence: The pot life can be influenced by the ambient temperature of your workspace. Higher temperatures generally accelerate the curing process and shorten the pot life, while lower temperatures can slow it down. So, if your workspace is warm, you'll need to work more quickly, while cooler conditions might give you a bit more time.

3. Exothermic Reaction: When you mix the resin and hardener, a chemical reaction occurs. This reaction generates heat, which is known as an exothermic reaction. The heat can further accelerate the curing process and shorten the pot life, especially in larger quantities of epoxy.

4. Indicators of Expiry: As the pot life nears its end, you might notice the mixture becoming thicker and harder to spread smoothly. It might also become cloudy or develop a "stringy" texture. These are signs that the epoxy is starting to cure and should no longer be used for your project.

5. Planning: To make the most of the pot life, plan your project accordingly. Have all your tools, materials, and surfaces ready before you start mixing the epoxy. This will help you work efficiently and avoid wasting precious time during application.

6. Small Batches: If you're working on a larger project, consider dividing the job into smaller sections and mixing epoxy in smaller batches. This way, you can maintain better control over the application and prevent wastage.

The pot life is a critical aspect of working with epoxy resin, especially when just learning the medium. Always double-check the instructions provided by the manufacturer and practice a bit to get a feel for how the epoxy behaves within its specified pot life in your particular working environment.

Bubbles

Air bubbles can form in epoxy resin for a variety of reasons. Understanding these reasons can help you take preventive measures and address them effectively.

These are how bubbles look in resin when the resin in still in liquid form.

Air bubbles can occur in resin for many different reasons. Stirring or mixing epoxy resin and hardener too vigorously can introduce air into the mixture. When you whip air into the liquid, it gets trapped as the epoxy starts to cure. Pouring epoxy too quickly onto a surface can create turbulence that traps air beneath the epoxy layer. Air can also become trapped in porous materials, such as wood, fabric, or uneven surfaces. When the epoxy is applied over these materials, the air has a tendency to escape, forming bubbles.

Applying epoxy on vertical surfaces can cause air to rise through the liquid and form bubbles as the epoxy starts to cure. Applying epoxy with a brush or spatula in a forceful manner can introduce air bubbles into the epoxy layer.

In addition, changes in temperature can cause air trapped within the epoxy mixture to expand. As the epoxy cures and solidifies, the expanding air creates bubbles. Pouring thick layers of epoxy can generate heat and increase the chances of air being trapped within the mixture. The chemical reaction that occurs when epoxy resin and hardener are mixed also generates heat. This heat can cause any trapped air to expand rapidly, creating bubbles within the curing epoxy.

Tip #39: If you're doing a deep pour or coating, consider pouring epoxy in thin layers rather than all at once.

This gives trapped air more chances to escape. Bubbles can also be caused by your workspace or your environment. Moisture or humidity in the environment can contribute to the formation of bubbles. Water vapor can create tiny air pockets within the epoxy as it cures. In your workspace, surfaces that are not properly cleaned, degreased, or sealed can trap air between the epoxy and the material, leading to bubbles.

It's important to mix epoxy gently to minimize the occurrence of air bubbles, apply it carefully, and address potential air trap points. Using techniques like a heat gun/torch, blowing on the surface, and creating thin layers can help release the trapped air. Practice and experience will also help you anticipate and manage potential bubble issues as you work with epoxy resin.

I know it sounds like having bubbles in your resin is inevitable, and it is important to remember that some minor imperfections are normal in epoxy projects. They can even add character to your finished piece. Dealing with air bubbles can be a skill that improves with practice. Don't get discouraged if you encounter bubbles in your initial attempts. With time, you'll become more adept at preventing and managing them.

There are many ways to deal with bubbles to ensure your finished art pieces are clear and solid.

One way is to set up your workspace in a clean, dust-free environment. This helps prevent debris from getting trapped in the epoxy and causing bubbles.

Tip #40: Make sure your mixing containers and stirring tools are clean and dry before using them.

When mixing the epoxy resin and hardener, stir slowly and gently to minimize the introduction of air into the mixture.

Tip #41: Avoid aggressive or rapid stirring, as it can whip air into the epoxy.

Placing the epoxy resin and hardener bottles in warm water before mixing can help reduce the viscosity of the components, making it easier for air bubbles to rise and escape during mixing.

After pouring the epoxy onto your surface or into your mold, use a heat gun or a lighter to remove air bubbles.

Tip #42: Keep the heat source moving in a sweeping motion above the surface to avoid overheating the epoxy or damaging the silicone mold.

Here is an air bubble before the heat gun is used.

Here are the air bubbles popped by the heat.

Sometimes, larger bubbles will rise to the surface on their own as the epoxy starts to cure. You can then use a toothpick or a pin to carefully pop these bubbles.

Tip #43: Periodically check the epoxy as it cures.

If you notice any new bubbles forming, you can use the techniques mentioned above to address them.

Chapter Summary

Let's take a moment to go over what we've covered in this chapter to make sure you have a good understanding of mixing ratios and times, as well as resin working times.

By reading this chapter, you have learned about the following:

- the importance of using the proper ratios
- common mixing ratios
- the time you should take to mix your resin
- what working time is
- the "pot life" of resin
- how air bubbles occur
- how you can prevent and deal with air bubble

Chapter 5: Using Molds

Silicone Molds

Silicone molds are a highly valued tool in the world of art projects due to their remarkable properties. These molds are crafted from flexible and durable silicone material, enabling them to easily capture intricate details and shapes.

This picture shows the flexibility of silicone.

Their non-stick nature ensures that once your creation is set, it can be effortlessly removed without any damage. This quality makes silicone molds particularly well-suited for delicate items, such as jewelry or sculptures, where preserving fine features is crucial. Silicone molds come in various shapes and sizes, offering artists a diverse range of options to explore. Whether replicating nature's designs or crafting abstract forms, silicone molds provide a dependable means to realize your artistic visions with precision and ease.

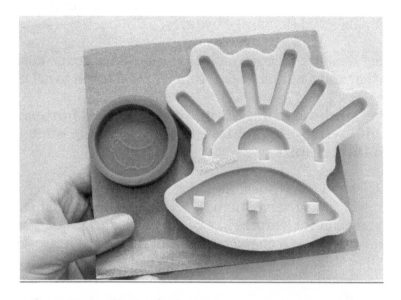

Here is an example of two silicone molds I use frequently.

Tip #44: When buying molds, clear silicone often indicates the molds are mass-produced, while colored silicone molds are often handmade.

Handmade molds often last longer than mass-made molds.

Silicone molds offer artists an array of textured effects that can greatly enhance the visual and tactile appeal of their art projects. The flexibility of silicone molds allows them to capture even the most intricate details, making it possible to replicate various textures with stunning accuracy.

Here are some textured effects that can be achieved using silicone molds:

1. Natural Textures: Silicone molds excel at capturing the textures found in nature, such as the intricate patterns on leaves, the rugged surface of tree bark, or the delicate veins on petals. This ability to replicate organic textures adds a lifelike quality to art pieces.

2. Geometric Patterns: Silicone molds come in a variety of shapes, including those with geometric patterns like triangles, squares, and hexagons. These molds allow artists to create sleek, modern designs with clean lines and structured textures.

3. Abstract Designs: Silicone molds can be used to create abstract textures that add a unique and unconventional touch to art pieces.

Tip #45: Combine different mold shapes and patterns. By doing this, artists can achieve unique, visually engaging, and dynamic results.

4. Industrial and Mechanical Elements: For those interested in steampunk or industrial aesthetics, silicone molds can help replicate mechanical textures like gears, bolts, and rivets. These textures add depth and character to art pieces with a futuristic or vintage vibe.

5. Textured Backgrounds: Silicone molds can also be utilized to create textured backgrounds or base layers for art projects. By incorporating textures like holographic coverings, drusy effects, waves, swirls, or stippling, artists can establish visually intriguing foundations for their creations.

This holographic effect was made using a silicone mold that has a holographic covering.

Tip #46: Do not put clear coats on textured resin pieces. Clear coats will hide the effect given by the silicone.

6. Faux Stone or Wood Effects: Silicone molds can mimic the textures of natural materials like stone or wood, allowing artists to create sculptures, jewelry, or decorative items that look convincingly like these materials.

7. Casting from Real Objects: Artists can press real objects, such as fabrics, leaves, or even seashells, into silicone molds to transfer their textures onto the resin. This technique adds a sense of realism and personal touch to the final piece.

Tip #47: Press the objects when the resin has been left to cure but is still soft. I recommend pressing after 3-4 hours.

8. Combining Textures: One of the most exciting aspects of working with silicone molds is the ability to combine different textures within a single piece. By layering textures or mixing mold designs, artists can craft visually complex and captivating art.

In essence, silicone molds serve as a versatile canvas for capturing a wide range of textures that can elevate the visual and tactile experience of art projects. This unique capability enables artists to experiment with various textures and create pieces that are truly one-of-a-kind.

In addition to their ability to capture intricate textures, silicone molds offer several other benefits that make them a popular choice for various art projects. Silicone molds are highly durable and can withstand repeated use without losing their shape or effectiveness. This durability ensures that your molds will last for a long time, making them a cost-effective investment. These molds are incredibly flexible, which makes it easy to release the cured material without causing any damage. This flexibility also allows for intricate designs with undercuts and delicate details that might be challenging with other mold materials.

Tip #48: With detailed molds, you can paint the details onto the mold before pouring. When you unmold your piece, the paint will have stuck to the hardened resin.

Silicone molds can handle high temperatures, making them suitable for a wide range of casting materials, including resin, wax, soap, and low-temperature metals. This versatility allows artists to experiment with different materials and techniques.

Tip #49: Never hold a direct heat source to your silicone molds. While silicone can handle high heat, direct application can result in damaged molds.

Silicone molds come in a wide variety of shapes, sizes, and designs. This versatility provides artists with numerous options to choose from and encourages creativity by enabling the creation of diverse and unique art pieces. As they are relatively affordable, they are accessible to artists of varying budgets and are often considered for their longevity and the number of casts they can produce. They can be easily washed with soap and water to remove any residue from previous casts.

Tip #50: Baking silicone molds can be used for resin. As baking silicone molds are made to withstand high heat as well, they are perfect for creative resin work.

In summary, silicone molds offer a host of advantages, such as durability, flexibility, ease of use, and the ability to work with various materials. These benefits make them indispensable tools for artists seeking to achieve high-quality and intricate results in their creative epoxy resin projects.

Handmade Molds

Using handmade molds for resin projects, created with molding clay and a plastic bottom covering, is a versatile and customizable approach in the world of crafting. This technique involves crafting a mold tailored to your specific design using molding clay, often referred to as modeling clay or polymer clay, and adding a plastic bottom for stability. Here's how the process generally works:

1. Design and Sculpt: Begin by sculpting your desired outline using molding clay. This could be an intricate design; it could have a texture or any form you'd like to cast with resin. The molding clay allows you to bring your creative vision to life with precision.

Tip #51: Outline your design in pencil or marker before creating your clay border.

2. Plastic Bottom: Once you're satisfied with your clay outline, create a stable base for your mold by adding a plastic bottom. This can be achieved by attaching a piece of plastic, such as a plastic sheet, to the underside of your clay design. The plastic adds support to your mold and ensures that the resin doesn't leak out during the casting process.

Tip #52: Use garbage bags. As garbage bags are plastic and glossy, they are great for both adding a barrier to your mold and giving your piece some shine.

3. Sealing and Prepping: It's important to ensure that the edges where the clay and plastic meet are properly sealed to prevent any potential leaks. This can be done by gently pressing and smoothing the edges together. You may also consider adding a layer of mold release agent to the clay to facilitate easy release of the resin once it cures.

4. Casting: Once your handmade mold is prepped and sealed, it's ready for casting. Mix your resin according to the manufacturer's instructions and carefully pour it into your mold. Use a toothpick or a heat tool to help release any air bubbles that may form.

5. Curing: Allow the resin to cure according to the recommended curing time. This typically ranges from several hours to a day, depending on the resin type and brand.

Tip #53: Check your piece frequently to ensure your mold has held. You do not want to go back to your piece in 72 hours to find a hardened mess.

6. Demolding: After the resin has fully cured, gently peel away the plastic and carefully flex the mold to release the cast resin piece. The plastic bottom will have helped maintain the mold's shape and prevent distortion during the casting process.

Using handmade molds with molding clay and a plastic bottom covering offers several advantages. You have complete control over the design and shape of your mold, allowing you to create unique and intricate pieces. This method allows you to experiment with various shapes, textures, and sizes, giving you endless creative possibilities. Handmade molds add a personal touch to your resin projects, showcasing your artistic style and attention to detail. Crafting your own molds can be cost-effective compared to purchasing pre-made molds, especially if you're creating a specific shape or design.

These molds also add a personal touch to your resin projects, showcasing your artistic style and attention to detail.

Creating your own molds is a learning experience that can enhance your crafting skills and understanding of mold-making techniques.

Tip #54: Practice makes perfect.

When using this approach, keep in mind that experimenting and practicing will help you refine your molding skills over time. As you become more familiar with the process, you'll be able to create molds that perfectly complement your resin artwork.

3D Molds

Making use of 3D molds and epoxy resin when crafting art is a popular approach for creating intricate patterns. I enjoy the potentials the molds yield, with my floral statues being one of my favorite projects to work on. This section will explain how to combine 3D silicone molds with epoxy resin.

These are two floral statues made with epoxy resin and dried flowers.

First, you have to select a mold that suits your artistic vision. Silicone molds are a common choice for 3D pieces due to their flexibility, ease of release, and ability to capture fine details. Ensure that the mold is clean, dry, and free of any debris or residue that could affect the quality of the final piece. Apply a mold release agent or a light coating of mold conditioner to prevent epoxy resin from sticking to the mold. This step is crucial to ensure easy demolding once the resin has cured.

Tip #55: If you do not have mold release on hand, use soap and water to release your piece from the mold after it is fully cured.

Once your resin is ready, carefully pour the mixed epoxy resin into the mold. Start with a thin layer to coat the mold's surface and eliminate air bubbles that might be trapped in intricate details. Use a heat gun or torch to gently remove any surface bubbles that appear. Depending on your design, you can embed various elements like dried flowers, beads, or small objects into the resin at this stage. Alternatively, you can pour multiple layers of resin to create a multidimensional effect. Allow each layer to partially cure before adding the next one.

Follow the epoxy resin's recommended curing time before attempting to demold. Once the resin has fully cured, carefully flex or twist the mold to release the cured piece. If you encounter resistance, avoid forcing the piece out to prevent damaging either the mold or the artwork.

Tip #56: Do not be after to bend your mold. Silicone is made to be flexible. You will not break it.

After demolding, you might need to trim any excess resin or clean up the edges to achieve your desired final shape. Sanding, polishing, and adding additional layers of clear resin for a glossy finish are common techniques to enhance the appearance of your art piece.

This is the 3D mold filled with resin.

Tip #57: Nail files make for great aids in sanding the edges of resin pieces.

Keep in mind that even after demolding, epoxy resin can continue to cure and strengthen over time. Allow your art piece to cure in a clean, dust-free environment for an extended period to ensure optimal hardness and durability.

Using 3D molds opens up a world of creative possibilities. Experiment with different mold shapes, sizes, and designs. Combine multiple molds, layer colors, and incorporate various materials to achieve unique and stunning results.

Remember that working with epoxy resin requires careful attention to detail, patience, and practice. Take your time, be mindful of safety precautions, and enjoy the artistic process of creating captivating pieces with 3D molds and epoxy resin.

Flat Molds

The possibilities are endless when you create art projects with flat molds and epoxy resin. You can make coasters, trays, wall art, abstract paintings, and so much more! Not to mention the plethora of textured molds and molds with line work that let you explore with different design elements.

This artist is using a flat mold to create a coaster.

To help you get the most out of working with flat molds and epoxy resin, here's a guide on how to effectively use them in your projects:

Select a flat mold that suits your project's dimensions and design. These molds can be made of silicone, plastic, or other materials.

Tip #58: Ensure that the mold is clean, dry, and free of any debris that could affect the quality of the resin.

Apply a mold release agent or mold conditioner to ensure easy demolding once the epoxy resin has cured. This step is essential to prevent the resin from sticking to the mold.

Follow the manufacturer's instructions to accurately mix the epoxy resin and hardener. Use a measuring scale to achieve the correct resin-to-hardener ratio. If desired, add colorants, pigments, or other additives to achieve the desired effect.

Carefully pour the mixed epoxy resin into the flat mold. Start with a thin layer to coat the bottom evenly and eliminate air bubbles. You can use a spreader or brush to help distribute the resin evenly.

Tip #59: For a bubble-free piece, try spraying your mold with 99% alcohol. This will help pop bubbles as they form but have no effect on your finished piece.

You can create depth and visual interest by adding multiple layers of epoxy resin. Allow each layer to partially cure before adding the next one. During this process, you can embed various elements, create swirls, or add other effects to achieve the desired design.

After pouring the resin, use a heat gun or torch to remove surface bubbles. Gently pass the heat source over the resin, which will cause the bubbles to rise and pop.

Follow the epoxy resin's recommended curing time before attempting to demold. Once the resin has fully cured, gently flex or twist the mold to release the cured piece. Be patient and avoid forcing the piece out to prevent damage.

The beauty of flat molds and epoxy resin is that the creative possibilities are truly endless. With a little bit of patience and practice, you can create amazing art projects in no time! The key is to carefully measure your ingredients, use a mold release agent, and be patient when allowing the epoxy resin to cure. With these tips, you'll be able to create beautiful artwork for yourself or gifts for friends and family.

Working with Wood

Working with wood and epoxy resin in art projects combines the natural beauty of wood with the glossy, translucent qualities of resin. This technique allows you to create stunning and unique pieces that highlight both materials.

Here a resin artist applies colored resin to a slice of wood to create a coaster.

To effectively work with wood and epoxy resin for art projects, start by choosing a suitable type of wood for your project. Hardwoods like oak, walnut, and maple are popular choices due to their durability and appealing grain patterns. Ensure that the wood is properly dried and free from defects.

Tip #60: Always seal your wood. Wood naturally has air inside, and if you do not seal it prior to pouring your resin, air will creep through and create bubbles in your art.

Prepare the wood before you bring out any epoxy resin. Do this by sanding the wood surface to achieve a smooth finish and to open up the pores of the wood. This helps the resin bond more effectively. Once you've sanded and shaped your wooden piece to your desired look, it is critical that the wood is sealed completely. The wood exhales air naturally, so if epoxy resin is applied without sealing the wood first, air bubbles will form that can ruin the entire project. Therefore, it's important to make sure no air can escape before adding the resin.

When pouring resin onto the wood, use a spreader or brush to evenly distribute the resin over the wood. You can also tilt the wood to help the resin flow and cover the entire surface. A heat gun or torch can be used to remove surface bubbles. For more depth and dimension, consider pouring epoxy resin in layers. Allow each layer to partially cure before adding the next one. This technique is particularly useful for creating waves or other textured effects.

After the epoxy resin has fully cured, sand the surface to achieve a smooth finish. Begin with coarse grit and gradually work your way to finer grits. This step is essential to remove any imperfections and achieve a polished look.

Tip #61: Use polyurethane or lacquer. To enhance the wood's appearance and protect the epoxy resin, apply a clear finish, such as polyurethane or lacquer.

This helps prevent UV damage and adds to the longevity of your art piece.

Creating art projects with wood and epoxy resin offers a fantastic opportunity for creativity and experimentation. Whether you're making river tables, coasters, wall art, or jewelry, the combination of wood and epoxy resin can result in visually striking and impressive pieces that showcase your artistic skills.

Chapter Summary

This chapter on using molds in resin art covers various techniques for creating and using molds in resin art projects. It discusses the advantages and applications of each type of mold, such as silicone molds for intricate details and flexibility, handmade molds for customization, 3D molds for complex shapes, flat molds for larger surfaces, and wood molds for a natural aesthetic.

By reading this chapter, you have learned about the following:

- different kinds of molds and their uses
- which textured effects silicone molds can achieve
- how to make your own handmade mold
- the positives to using silicone molds for 3D creations
- how to use resin with wood

Chapter 6: The Curing Process

The Three Stages

Epoxy resin is a versatile and widely used synthetic material known for its strength, durability, and adhesive properties. One of the most critical stages in working with epoxy resin is the curing process. Curing is the chemical reaction that transforms the liquid epoxy resin into a solid, strong, and rigid material. This chapter delves into the intricacies of the epoxy resin curing process, its stages, factors influencing curing, and some common techniques used for successful epoxy curing.

Understanding the epoxy resin curing process is essential for achieving desired material properties and performance. Proper handling, temperature control, and adherence to manufacturer recommendations are critical for successful epoxy curing. Whether for artistic creations, structural applications, or industrial processes, mastering epoxy curing techniques is fundamental for achieving the best results.

The process of epoxy resin curing is a crucial step in achieving a strong and durable final product. This process involves the reaction of two primary components: the resin and the curing agent, commonly referred to as the hardener. The hardener typically contains active groups, such as amines or anhydrides, which react with the epoxy groups in the resin. This chemical reaction creates strong covalent bonds that are essential for the resin to solidify and harden.

Pictured here is epoxy resin and hardener. Part A and Part B

The process of curing epoxy resin can be divided into three stages, each with its own unique characteristics. The first stage is the induction period, which begins immediately after the resin and hardener are mixed together. During this stage, the mixture is still relatively fluid and has not yet started to solidify. The second stage is the exothermic reaction period, which is marked by a significant increase in temperature as the chemical reaction between the resin and hardener progresses. This stage is critical as it determines the final strength and durability of the cured epoxy resin. The third and final stage is the cooling period, during which the mixture gradually cools and solidifies into a hardened mass. Understanding the different stages of epoxy resin curing is essential for ensuring that the final product is of the highest quality. By carefully monitoring the temperature and timing of each stage, it is possible to achieve optimal curing and create a final product that is strong, durable, and resistant to damage.

Let's take a closer look at each stage together.

First Stage

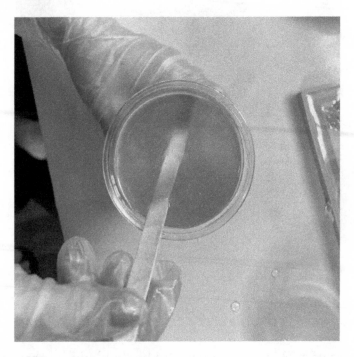

You can see this epoxy resin and hardener mixing together. You see how the liquid is cloudy?

The first stage of epoxy resin curing is known as the induction period or the "open time." This is when the epoxy is still in its liquid form. During this period, the resin and hardener are blended together to initiate a chemical reaction. The mixture remains workable in its liquid state during this first stage of solidifying. All manual tasks like molding, coloring, or assembly should be accomplished during this stage for long-lasting bonding effects later on. The open time is equivalent to the pot life of your resin.

The open time varies between different types of resins and hardeners but typically ranges from 5 minutes to an hour. It is important to note that the open time can vary significantly depending on environmental factors such as temperature, moisture content, and air pressure. Additionally, it is important to ensure that the ratio of resin to hardener is accurate for achieving optimal curing results.

Tip #62: Always plan for your pot life.

In order to take full advantage of this open time period, it is essential to plan ahead and understand how much working time you have before the mixture begins to thicken and solidify too much. Preparation for tasks like molding should be done in advance so they can be completed within the limited timeframe of the open time period. During this period, it is also important to keep an eye out for signs of premature hardening or curing (e.g., small white spots or dimples), which may indicate that your mixture has started solidifying and needs stirring again before continuing with any further tasks.

Once the open time period has passed, it is essential to begin the exothermic reaction period immediately in order for optimal curing performance and properties later on.

Second Stage

The second stage of epoxy curing is known as the exothermic reaction period. This is when the resin and hardener begin to heat up and start chemically reacting with each other, causing the mixture to thicken and take on a gel-like form. The exothermic reaction period typically lasts for around 60 minutes; however, this timeframe can be affected by a variety of factors, including temperature, air pressure, moisture content, and the ratio of resin to hardener that was used in the mix. During this stage, it is important to monitor the temperature of the epoxy as it rises.

Tip #63: Wear a mask.

If around your resin during this period, make sure to wear a mask to protect yourself against the toxicity of the fumes released.

Tip #64: Minimize the movement of your resin piece during this period.

Any movement of the piece could result in a damaged or ruined project.

During this exothermic reaction period, the epoxy mixture will become increasingly viscous until it eventually reaches a point where it can no longer be handled without protective gloves. The mixture will also begin to take on a slightly milky appearance due to its increased viscosity. At this point, manual tasks such as molding or assembly should not be attempted since they may disrupt the curing process and cause premature hardening or improper bonding later on.

Tip #65: Mix slowly.

In order to ensure you do not speed up or activate this period prematurely, mix your resin slowly when combining your two agents and when adding colorants.

Third Stage

The third and final stage of epoxy curing is the cooling period. This is when the epoxy reaches its full strength and durability. During this time, the epoxy must be kept away from extreme temperatures and moist environments in order to attain optimal performance properties. The duration of this stage depends on many factors, such as temperature, air humidity, etc., but typically takes several days.

Tip #66: Walk away.

Resist the temptation to play with your piece. I know it's hard, but at this point, you must let the resin cure in peace.

During the cooling period, it is important to monitor your project closely for any signs of cracking or uneven curing that may indicate that either too much or too little heat was used during the exothermic reaction period. If these problems occur, it can be difficult to fix them without damaging your finished product in the process.

It is also important to remember that during the cooling period, your epoxy may still be a bit flexible (depending on the formulation). This flexibility means that the epoxy may need extra support while it hardens in order to avoid any damage due to heavy loads or pressure being applied before it has had time to fully cure and harden.

Tip #67: Always cure on level surfaces.

During this period, it is crucial to ensure your resin is level. Any unevenness will be permanently visible in your finished piece.

Once your epoxy has cooled off completely, it should attain maximum strength and bond durability. Your project will then be ready for use!

Curing Times

Resin curing time refers to the period it takes for a liquid resin to transform from a liquid state to a solid state. This process, known as "curing," involves chemical reactions that create strong molecular bonds within the resin, resulting in a hardened material.

The time it takes for resin to harden can vary depending on a few factors. Different types of resins have unique curing properties and need specific conditions, temperatures, and times before they are set. Some resins require special catalysts or hardening agents in order to start the curing process, and the amount of catalyst used affects how long it takes for the resin to cure. Recipes must be followed correctly when measuring ingredients since incorrect measurements can extend the curing process. Temperature is also very important for resin hardening; cool weather slows down the curing time while heat accelerates it. Humidity may give certain resins trouble if the moisture levels are too high and cause incomplete curing or surface imperfections.

Tip #68: Humidifiers in your workspace can greatly help your piece cure.

Resin layers that are thicker than average take longer for the heat generated during curing to dissipate. UV light is also necessary for some resins to cure, which means that the intensity and wavelength generated by the UV light source influence how quickly the resin sets. Last but not least, additives like pigments, fillers, and stabilizers impact curing speed.

Resin is a tricky material; it requires patience and precision in order to be manipulated successfully. But when working with it, it is hard to resist meddling with your piece before it is completely cured. I often like to work in the afternoon or evening so that the piece sets while I sleep. The first 12 hours of the curing process are the most sensitive, and any fiddling can have permanent effects on the piece.

Tip #69: Write it down.

Note how long each of your molds or projects takes to cure so you know what to expect next time.

Curing Temperature

Curing temperatures are crucial when working with epoxy resin for art projects, as they can significantly impact the curing process and the final outcome of your creations.

Most epoxy resins used in art projects have a recommended temperature range for optimal curing. This range is typically between 70°F to 80°F (21°C to 27°C). Working within this range ensures that the resin cures correctly and uniformly. It's important to note that curing time and temperature are interrelated. As temperature increases, the epoxy resin will cure faster; as temperature decreases, it will cure slower. However, it's essential to maintain a consistent temperature to ensure even curing and avoid potential issues.

Tip #70: A heating mat or chamber can help your pieces cure more quickly.

Avoid curing epoxy resin in extremely hot or cold environments. Extreme heat can accelerate curing to the point of creating bubbles and warping. In contrast, extreme cold can lead to incomplete curing and surface defects. If you're working in a colder environment, epoxy resin can take longer to cure or might not cure properly. Cold temperatures slow down the chemical reactions responsible for curing. To counter this, you can warm the resin, hardener, and workspace to the recommended temperature range using methods like space heaters or heat lamps.

While not directly related to temperature, proper ventilation is essential during curing.

Epoxy resins often release volatile organic compounds (VOCs) as they cure. Adequate ventilation helps dissipate these fumes and prevents them from being trapped in the resin.

UV-curable epoxy resins are a subset of epoxy resins that cure under ultraviolet light exposure. These resins offer rapid curing times and are ideal for small art projects.

When using UV-curable epoxy resin, ensure you have a UV light source that matches the resin's specifications for intensity and wavelength.

You can use various ways to control the temperature while working on epoxy resin art projects. If possible, work in a space where you can control the temperature to fall within the recommended range. Use heaters to raise the temperature or fans to lower it as needed.

To ensure proper mixing and consistent curing, warm the epoxy resin and hardener to the desired temperature before combining them. Consider using a thermometer to monitor the workspace temperature and ensure it remains steady throughout the curing process.

Understanding the significance of recommended temperatures and taking steps to control and maintain them can enhance your epoxy resin art projects' quality, durability, and overall success.

Chapter Summary

This chapter delves into the crucial aspects of resin curing in the context of resin art. It breaks down the process into three stages, explaining how each stage contributes to the final result. The chapter explores the significance of proper curing times and temperatures in achieving optimal resin hardness and clarity. It offers insights into the factors that influence curing, such as the type of resin used and environmental conditions. By providing practical guidance on selecting appropriate curing times and temperatures, this chapter equips artists with the knowledge to create resin artworks with the desired strength and aesthetic appeal.

From this chapter, you should now have a better understanding on:

- the three stages of curing
- what occurs during the curing process
- the cooling period
- how long resin takes to cure
- how heat affects resin during the curing process
- how to use resin with wood

Chapter 7: Adding Color

Resin is such an amazing tool to use as an artist. Using color with resin can open so many more artistic possibilities. Depending on the artist's creativity, there will be no limit to the kinds of artwork they can create. From deep blue oceans to lush green forests, or brilliant red sunsets, all of these can be created with color and resin.

When it comes to adding color to resin, it's important to choose the appropriate medium for your project. For example, if you're looking for a vibrant and bold look that will really stand out, then using craft pigments such as mica powders might be the best option. These pigments come in a wide variety of colors and are specially formulated for use with resin projects, so they won't fade or change over time as other dyes or paints might. Alternatively, alcohol ink can also be used as well and provides an even more dynamic range of colors than just mica powders. The differences between these two products really come down to personal preference in terms of finish and vibrancy.

Tip #71: Experiment. Experiment with all forms of colorants to find your favorites. You never know what you will end up loving or what works best for you without trying.

If you're looking to achieve a softer and more subtle look, then using resin tints may be the best choice. These tints are specially formulated for use in resin and come in various shades of primary colors. They can also be mixed together to create different hues and tones that you may not find with mica powders or alcohol ink. This is great for creating delicate pastel palettes or soft gradients – perfect for creating a dreamy landscape or other nature-themed projects.

No matter the type of color product used, there are some basic techniques to keep in mind when using color with epoxy resin. The most important aspect is ensuring that you mix the pigment thoroughly into the resin before pouring it into your mold or onto your surface. This will help ensure that the colors stay even throughout and eliminate any streaks or uneven spots from forming during curing time. Additionally, it's important to measure out your pigment amounts carefully so as not to overpower the color of the resin, as too much pigment can end up creating a murky-looking piece.

Tip #72: Mix until the color is all the way to the bottom. Leave no clear resin behind.

With a little practice and experimentation, you'll be able to create beautiful works of art with epoxy resin and color that will last for years to come. So, get creative and have fun!

Mica Powders

This resin ashtray was made using mica powder as a colorant. Look how the mica powder adds texture to this piece.

Mica powders are a great way to really bring a project to life. Their reflective properties and their ability to subtly blend different colors together give them an edge over most other craft pigments. They can be used with epoxy resin to create marbled effects or be used alone for a more solid finish. I find that often mica powder also gives that shimmery effect.

Mica powder offers a range of effects that can add depth, shine, and a touch of elegance to your resin creations.

Here are some effects you can achieve using mica powder:

1. Pearlescent Sheen: Mica powder imparts a pearlescent or metallic sheen to the resin, creating a lustrous and shimmering surface that changes appearance with varying angles of light.

2. Color Shifting: Some mica powders have color-shifting properties, meaning they appear to change color depending on the angle of light. This effect can add an intriguing and magical quality to your resin pieces.

3. Opaque and Translucent Layers: Depending on the concentration of mica powder used, you can create layers that vary in opacity and translucency. This allows you to craft pieces with intricate depth and visual interest.

4. Gradient and Ombré Effects: By gradually mixing different shades of mica powder into your resin, you can achieve beautiful gradient and ombré effects. This works particularly well for projects like jewelry where a smooth color transition is desired.

5. Texture and Patterns: Mica powder can be manipulated within the resin to create textured or patterned effects. You can swirl, blend, or layer different colors to achieve intricate patterns reminiscent of natural materials like stone or agate.

6. Faux Gemstone Imitation: Mica powder can be used to mimic the appearance of gemstones, such as opals or quartz, by creating a captivating play of colors and light within the resin.

7. Highlighting and Accents: Mica powder can be strategically applied to certain areas of your resin piece to create focal points, highlight details, or add accents to your design.

8. Mixed Media: Mica powder can be combined with other additives like glitter, pigments, or even dried flowers to achieve multi-dimensional and eye-catching effects.

Using mica powders is relatively easy - simply add the powder into the resin, making sure that it is blended in thoroughly before pouring it into your mold or onto your surface. The amount of powder you add will depend on how vibrant you want the color to be, so it's important to measure carefully and experiment with different ratios until you get the desired effect.

The powders can be added directly to the resin mix in a relatively small quantity - typically between 1-2% of the total volume of resin - depending on how strong a color you would like to achieve. Start off with a smaller amount and then add more if needed.

Tip #73: Add a little powder at a time.

By going little by little, you will be able to get to your desired color without overpowering your resin.

It's important to ensure that the mica powder is completely mixed into the resin before it is poured into your mold or onto your surface, as this will help prevent any uneven spots from forming during curing time. Additionally, when using mica powder, it's best to wear gloves and work in a ventilated area so as not to inhale any particles or residue from the pigment.

This is how most mica powders come packaged.

Here are some helpful steps for mixing mica powder into resin:

1. Prepare Your Resin: Mix your epoxy resin according to the manufacturer's instructions. Make sure it's thoroughly mixed to avoid any streaks or unevenness.

2. Add Mica Powder: Gradually add a small amount of mica powder to your mixed resin. The amount will depend on how intense you want the color and shimmer effect to be. Start with a small amount and gradually add more until you achieve the desired effect.

3. Mix Thoroughly: Gently stir the mica powder into the resin using a stirring stick or spatula. Be sure to mix it thoroughly to ensure even distribution. Avoid over-stirring, which can introduce air bubbles.

Here the artist is mixing in white mica powder with the clear resin.

4. Check Color: Before pouring the resin into your mold or project, check the color under proper lighting conditions. Mica powder can

appear differently in different lighting, so make sure you're happy with the color before proceeding.

5. Pour Resin: Carefully pour the resin into your mold or project. If you're creating a layered effect, you can pour a thin layer, let it partially cure, and then add more layers with mica powder for depth.

6. Manipulate Effects: If desired, you can manipulate the mica powder within the resin using tools like toothpicks or small brushes to create patterns, swirls, or other effects.

7. Cure: Allow the resin to cure according to the manufacturer's instructions. This typically involves letting it sit undisturbed for a specified period of time. Keep an eye out for any air bubbles that may rise to the surface during curing.

8. Finish: Once the resin has fully cured, you can remove it from the mold and do any necessary finishing touches, such as sanding and polishing, to achieve the desired look.

Using mica powder in your projects adds a new level of creativity and vibrancy that can turn any work of art into something truly special. From vibrant seascapes with shimmering blue waves to stunning sunsets where every hue of pink, orange, and yellow comes alive - these are just some of the many amazing works you can create with mica powder and epoxy resin.

Alcohol Inks

Alcohol ink is a highly pigmented and fast-drying liquid dye that is used for various art and craft projects but is especially magical when used in resin art. It's known for its vibrant colors, fluidity, and ability to create stunning abstract designs.

Tip #74: Play first with water.

Alcohol ink is an extremely playful medium and tends to take some practice. A budget-friendly way to experiment is to play with dropping the color in water.

Alcohol inks are composed of dye colorants suspended in an alcohol solvent. The alcohol base allows the inks to spread easily, blend, and interact with various surfaces. Their versatility makes them a popular choice for mixed media art, resin art, and other crafts.

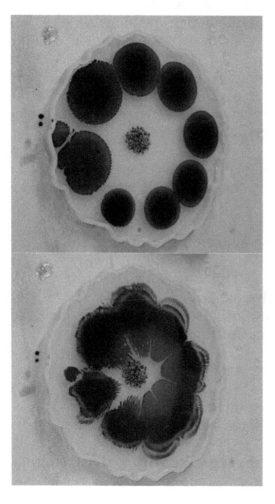

In these two photos, you can easily see how alcohol ink spreads in resin.

Alcohol inks are known for their intense and vibrant colors. They come in a wide spectrum of shades, from bright and bold to soft and pastel. One of the unique qualities of alcohol inks is their ability to blend seamlessly together. When mixed with resin, they quickly spread and interact, creating beautiful color transitions and gradients. This makes them ideal for creating smooth, fluid designs.

Alcohol inks tend to flow and move when applied to a surface. This characteristic allows artists to achieve dynamic, unpredictable patterns that can resemble natural elements like water or marble. Multiple layers of alcohol ink can be applied to one resin layer, with each drop of color interacting and blending with the others beneath. This makes it possible to create intricate and complex designs.

Artists often use various tools to manipulate alcohol inks, such as brushes, droppers, air blowers, and palette knives. Techniques like dripping, splattering, and blowing air across the ink can yield interesting textures and patterns.

When using alcohol ink in resin, you can achieve a variety of captivating effects that add depth, movement, and visual interest to your creations.

Here are some common effects you can create:

1. Marbling: Alcohol inks are known for their ability to create beautiful, marbled patterns within resin. The inks tend to blend and flow together, producing a swirling, marble-like effect that can be both mesmerizing and unpredictable.

2. Cell Formation: Alcohol inks can interact with the resin in such a way that they create cells, which are small, round, and often translucent areas with distinct edges. This effect can resemble the appearance of cells in natural materials like stone or agate.

Tip #75: Blow on the inks with a straw to help cell formation.

3. Color Blending: By combining different colors of alcohol ink, you can achieve smooth color transitions and gradients. This effect is

particularly striking when using complementary or analogous colors.

4. Abstract Designs: Alcohol inks give you the freedom to create abstract designs that are both vibrant and fluid. You can experiment with different pouring techniques, tilting the mold or using various tools to manipulate the inks and resin into unique shapes and patterns.

5. Opaque and Transparent Layers: Depending on the opacity of the alcohol ink and the amount used, you can create layers of varying transparency. This can result in an intriguing interplay of colors and textures.

6. Landscapes and Nature-Inspired Scenes: With careful use of alcohol inks and manipulation techniques, you can mimic natural elements such as landscapes, skies, and water bodies. The flowing nature of alcohol inks lends itself well to creating these types of scenes.

7. Iridescent and Metallic Effects: Some alcohol inks have metallic or iridescent properties that, when combined with resin, can add a stunning sheen and depth to your projects.

Remember that alcohol inks are quite dynamic and can behave differently depending on factors like the brand of alcohol ink, the type of resin used, the pouring technique, and the surface you're working on. It's a good idea to experiment on small surfaces or test pieces before attempting larger projects to understand how the inks interact with the resin.

By exploring different techniques and combinations, you can create truly unique and visually captivating resin art that showcases the beauty of alcohol ink effects.

Here's how to use alcohol ink in resin:

1. Prepare Your Resin: Just like when using mica powder, start by preparing your epoxy resin according to the manufacturer's instructions. Make sure it's mixed thoroughly and any air bubbles are removed.

2. Choose Your Alcohol Inks: Select the alcohol ink colors you want to use. Alcohol inks come in a wide range of colors and can be mixed to create custom shades.

3. Add Alcohol Inks: Using a dropper or similar tool, add drops of alcohol ink directly into the mixed resin. You can add a few drops of one color or experiment with multiple colors to create intricate designs.

4. Mix Gently: Use a stirring stick or spatula to gently swirl and mix the alcohol ink into the resin. The alcohol in the ink will interact with the resin, creating unique patterns and color dispersion.

5. Pour Resin: Carefully pour the resin with alcohol ink into your mold or project. You can pour it in a single layer or create layered effects by allowing each layer to partially cure before adding more resin.

6. Manipulate Effects: Similar to using mica powder, you can use tools like toothpicks, brushes, or even a gentle puff of air to manipulate and spread the alcohol ink patterns within the resin.

7. Cure: Allow the resin to cure based on the manufacturer's instructions. Keep an eye out for any air bubbles that might form during the curing process.

8. Finish: Once the resin has fully cured, you can remove it from the mold and perform any necessary finishing steps, such as sanding, polishing, and sealing.

Paint

Using paint in conjunction with epoxy resin offers artists a versatile and captivating way to create art. Epoxy resin's glossy and transparent finish enhances the visual depth and vibrancy of paint colors, resulting in a striking three-dimensional effect. This technique allows for intricate layering, blending, and texture manipulation, as artists can apply acrylic or oil paints to the resin surface before it cures. By carefully controlling the viscosity of the paint and the resin, artists can achieve captivating visual effects such as fluid gradients, abstract patterns, and dynamic textures. The interplay between the translucent resin and opaque paint creates a sense of depth and movement that traditional two-dimensional art often lacks. Whether it's encapsulating pigments within the resin layers or painting directly onto the cured surface, the combination of epoxy resin and paint unlocks a realm of artistic possibilities, enabling creators to produce stunning, multi-dimensional pieces that engage the viewer's senses in a unique and immersive manner.

Combining epoxy resin and paint offers artists an avenue to experiment with various techniques and effects. One popular approach is the "dirty pour" method, where multiple paint colors are mixed and poured onto the resin-coated surface. As the resin cures, the colors blend and interact in captivating ways, resulting in intricate patterns and organic designs. Additionally, you can embed objects like dried flowers, metallic foils, or even small trinkets within the resin layers, further enhancing the visual appeal and texture of the artwork.

Controlling the opacity and translucency of the paint also adds a level of complexity. By using transparent or semi-transparent paints, artists can create a sense of depth by allowing light to pass through the layers, while opaque paints can be employed to build up more solid and defined elements. The combination of these techniques allows artists like you to create artworks that evolve as light interacts with them, revealing different layers and hidden details from various angles.

The marriage of epoxy resin and paint opens the door to endless creative possibilities, enabling artists to produce visually captivating and emotionally engaging artworks that push the boundaries of traditional two-dimensional art. Whether the goal is to achieve vibrant abstract compositions, realistic landscapes with added depth, or unique mixed-media pieces, the combination of epoxy resin and paint continues to be a fascinating and dynamic technique in the world of contemporary art.

This plain acrylic paint is amazing when working with resin.

Here's how you can do it:

1. Gather Your Materials: You'll need epoxy resin, acrylic paint in the desired colors, mixing cups, mixing sticks, gloves, and your chosen project surface (e.g., a mold or canvas).

2. Prepare the Epoxy Resin: Follow the instructions provided with your epoxy resin kit to mix the resin and hardener in the correct proportions. Thoroughly stir the mixture according to the recommended stirring time.

3. Prepare the Acrylic Paint: Squeeze a small amount of acrylic paint into a separate mixing cup. Choose your desired paint colors and adjust the amount based on the intensity of color you want to achieve in the resin.

4. Mix Acrylic Paint into Epoxy Resin: Gradually add the acrylic paint to the mixed epoxy resin. Start with a small amount and mix thoroughly. You can adjust the color by adding more paint until you achieve the desired shade.

5. Stir Thoroughly: Mix the acrylic paint and epoxy resin together thoroughly. Stir gently to avoid introducing air bubbles. Make sure the color is evenly distributed throughout the mixture.

6. Test the Color: Before proceeding with your project, you can do a small test pour to see how the color appears once the resin cures. This allows you to make any necessary adjustments to the color or intensity.

7. Pour and Spread: Carefully pour the colored epoxy resin into your mold or onto your project surface. Use a clean, flat tool (like a spatula) to spread the resin evenly.

8. Pop Bubbles: If you notice any air bubbles rising to the surface, use a heat gun or torch to gently pass over the resin. This will help eliminate bubbles and create a smooth surface.

9. Curing Time: Allow the epoxy resin to cure according to the manufacturer's instructions. This can take several hours to a few days, depending on the type of resin used.

10. Finishing Touches: Once the resin is fully cured, you can sand, shape, or polish your project as needed to achieve the desired finish.

The intensity of the color may change slightly as the resin cures, so it's a good idea to do a test pour and observe how the color develops before applying it to your main project.

Chapter Summary

This chapter dives into the art of incorporating colorants into resin creations. It extensively covers three primary types of colorants: mica powder, alcohol inks, and paint. The chapter elucidates the unique properties and effects of each colorant, allowing artists to make informed choices based on their creative vision. It provides step-by-step instructions on how to properly mix and apply these colorants to resin, ensuring even distribution and captivating visual effects. Whether artists seek vibrant hues, subtle shimmers, or intricate patterns, this chapter empowers them to experiment and achieve captivating results by mastering the use of colorants in resin art.

From this chapter, you should now feel confident when:

- deciding which colorant best suits your project
- handling mica powders
- experimenting with dropping alcohol inks
- mixing colorants into your resin
- adding paint

Chapter 8: Using Add-Ins

Dried Flowers

Dried flowers offer a unique blend of nature's beauty and enduring charm. Through a meticulous process of dehydration, these delicate blooms are preserved, allowing them to retain their colors, shapes, and textures long after they've been plucked. Whether used in crafting, home decor, or even symbolic gestures, dried flowers have a timeless appeal that captures the essence of the natural world in a captivating and sustainable way.

Finding Dried Flowers

You can find dried flowers in various places, including craft stores, specialty floral shops, online marketplaces, and even some garden centers. They're also often available at farmers' markets and artisanal shops. Additionally, you can create your own dried flowers by carefully preserving blooms from your garden or bouquets.

Tip #76: Find cheap flowers to dry in parks, fields, or in your neighborhood.

These are how dried, pressed flowers look when bought.

These are some of my favorite places to find dried flowers, both online and offline:

1. Craft Stores: Many craft stores offer a selection of dried flowers specifically for crafting purposes. These stores often have a dedicated section for dried flowers, potpourri, and floral arrangements.

2. Floral Shops: Specialized floral shops or flower markets might carry dried flowers alongside fresh blooms. These shops can be a great place to find unique and exotic dried flower varieties.

3. Online Retailers: Numerous online marketplaces and retailers specialize in dried flowers for crafts.

Tip #77: Websites like Etsy, Amazon, and specialty floral supply stores offer a wide range of options that you can order and have delivered to your doorstep.

4. Farmers' Markets: Local farmers' markets sometimes feature dried flower vendors who sell bouquets, wreaths, and other dried floral arrangements.

5. Garden Centers: Some garden centers or nurseries may offer dried flowers or dried flower arrangements, especially during the off-season.

6. Artisanal Shops: Boutiques and artisanal shops that focus on home decor, gifts, and handmade goods may carry dried flower products or even offer workshops on creating crafts with dried flowers.

7. Online Flower Farms: Some online flower farms specialize in growing and selling dried flowers. These farms often have a wider variety of choices and may even allow you to customize your order.

Tip #78: Always check reviews when dealing with online merchants.

8. DIY: As mentioned earlier, you can also dry your own flowers from your garden or bouquets. This gives you the freedom to choose the flowers you want and to experiment with different drying methods.

When looking for dried flowers for crafts, consider the specific project you have in mind and the type of flowers that would work best. Whether you're aiming for a rustic, elegant, or vibrant look, you'll likely find a source that suits your creative needs.

Here the artist adjusts the position of the dried leaf with her stir stick.

Drying Flowers Yourself

Drying flowers yourself can be a rewarding and creative process. It can also be a way to preserve the beauty of a favorite flower for longer than its natural lifespan. To dry your flowers, start by gathering your materials. You'll need a container, a bowl of silica gel, and the flowers themselves. Carefully remove the leaves from the stems, leaving only the blooms.

Next, evenly spread out the flowers in the container. Sprinkle silica gel over the flowers, making sure to get enough on each one. Gently shake the container to ensure that the silica gel is completely distributed. Place the container in a well-ventilated area.

Let the flowers sit in the container for at least two weeks. Once they are completely dry, lightly brush off any excess silica gel, and you will have beautiful flowers to enjoy for years to come.

If you don't have access to silica gel, try following this method instead:

1. Choose the right flowers: Select flowers with petals that are relatively dry and not fully opened.

Tip #79: Flowers like roses, lavender, daisies, and baby's breath work well for drying.

2. Trim stems: Cut the stems to your desired length and remove any excess leaves.

3. Bundle flowers: Group a small number of flowers together and secure the stems with a rubber band or twine.

4. Hang upside down: Hang the flower bundles upside down in a cool, dark, and well-ventilated space. This allows the flowers to dry naturally and maintain their shape.

Tip #80: Make sure there's enough space between bundles to prevent mold growth.

5. Patience is key: Let the flowers hang for about 2-4 weeks, depending on the flower type and humidity levels. They should feel dry and papery to the touch.

6. Check and rearrange: Periodically check the flowers for any signs of mold or damage. If needed, rearrange the bundles to ensure even drying.

7. Display or store: Once dried, gently remove the rubber bands or twine and use the flowers in various creative projects, arrangements, or decor.

Remember, the drying time can vary based on factors like humidity and flower type. Experiment with different flowers and methods to find what works best for you.

Pressing Flowers

Pressing dried flowers is an age-old art that has been practiced for centuries. It is a wonderful way to capture a special moment and preserve a memory. The process is fairly simple and requires just a few tools and materials: some flowers, a heavy book, and a few sheets of thick white paper.

First, select your flowers. Make sure you choose those that are relatively dry and have been properly harvested. You don't want to press flowers that are still wet or damp, as this will make them deteriorate faster. Once you have your blooms, place them in between two sheets of white paper and then carefully sandwich them between the pages of a heavy book.

Next, make sure the book is closed tightly and weighed down with something heavy, such as a stack of books or a heavy object.

Tip #81: Using large textbooks or old phonebooks often does the trick.

Leave the flowers to press for about two weeks, making sure to check them every few days. You'll know they're ready when they feel dry and stiff to the touch.

Once pressed, the flowers can be used in a variety of craft projects. They can be used to embellish cards and scrapbook pages, make framed art, or embellish homemade gifts. Pressing flowers is a simple yet rewarding way to capture the beauty of nature for years to come. Enjoy!

Using with Resin

Using dried flowers with epoxy resin is a popular and creative way to incorporate natural elements into your crafts. Here are some steps for successfully working with dried flowers and epoxy resin:

1. Choose the Right Flowers: Opt for dried flowers that are relatively flat and thin, as they will be easier to embed in the resin. Flowers with thicker petals may not adhere as well or could create air pockets.

2. Prep the Flowers: Trim any excess stems and make sure the flowers are clean and free from dust.

Tip #82: Gently press the dried flowers beforehand to ensure they lie flat.

3. Prepare the Resin: Follow the manufacturer's instructions to mix the epoxy resin. Make sure to work in a well-ventilated area and wear appropriate protective gear, such as gloves and a mask.

4. Arrange the Flowers: Arrange the dried flowers in the desired pattern on your chosen surface. This could be a canvas, tray, coaster, or any other item you're embellishing with resin.

Tip #83: Pour a thin layer of epoxy resin into your mold or onto the surface before placing your flowers.

This helps anchor the flowers and prevents them from floating to the top when you add the remaining resin.

5. Place the Flowers: Gently place the dried flowers onto a resin layer. Use a toothpick or a small tool to adjust their position and ensure they're evenly spaced.

6. Complete the Pour: Slowly pour the rest of the epoxy resin over the dried flowers, making sure to cover them completely.

Tip #84: Use a toothpick to guide the resin around the flowers and eliminate any air bubbles.

7. Pop Bubbles: To remove air bubbles that may have formed, gently blow on the surface with a straw or use a heat gun on a low setting. Be careful not to overheat the resin, as this could cause it to crack or discolor.

8. Curing Time: Allow the resin to cure according to the manufacturer's instructions. This usually takes around 24 to 48 hours. Make sure your piece is in a dust-free environment during this time.

9. Finishing Touches: Once the resin is fully cured, you can sand the edges if needed and apply a clear sealant to enhance the glossy finish.

This is a gorgeous, finished tray made with epoxy resin and real dried flowers.

Vinyl Inserts and Stickers

Using vinyl inserts and stickers in resin artwork provides a multitude of design possibilities. With the integration of these elements, you can upgrade the overall look and make your work one-of-a-kind. Think about adding a famous quote, a compelling graphic, or even an intricate vinyl overlay that enhances the entire layout.

This approach allows for the addition of individual touches and extra layers of visual highlight, taking your resin artwork to an advanced level of style and uniqueness. The combination of resin's alluring transparency with the colorful and flexible character of vinyl inserts and stickers can bring out an exceptionally incredible masterpiece.

Here a vinyl overlay was used to create the appearance of cheetah print.

Here are the steps to add vinyl inserts or stickers to your resin art project:

1. Prepare Your Materials:

Gather all the necessary materials, including your resin mixture, vinyl inserts or stickers, a mixing cup, stirring sticks, a torch or heat gun (for removing bubbles), and any additional tools you might need.

2. Design Planning:

Decide where you want to place the vinyl inserts or stickers on your resin art piece. Plan the layout and arrangement to ensure a balanced and visually pleasing composition.

Tip #85: Place your vinyl on your mold prior to pouring to make sure you're pleased with the placement.

3. Prepare the Resin:

Mix your resin according to the manufacturer's instructions. Make sure to mix it thoroughly but avoid introducing air bubbles during the mixing process.

4. Apply a Base Layer:

Pour a thin layer of resin into your chosen canvas or mold. This will serve as the base layer for your artwork.

5. Position the Vinyl Inserts/Stickers:

Carefully place the vinyl inserts or stickers onto the wet resin surface.

Tip #86: Use a gentle touch when placing to ensure they adhere smoothly and without wrinkles.

6. Press and Seal:

Gently press down on the vinyl inserts or stickers to ensure proper adhesion and to eliminate any air bubbles trapped beneath them.

7. Add More Resin:

Pour the remaining resin mixture over the vinyl inserts or stickers. Use a stirring stick to guide the resin to cover the entire surface evenly.

8. Remove Bubbles:

To eliminate air bubbles that might have formed during the pouring process, use a torch or heat gun. Gently pass the flame over the surface but avoid overheating the resin.

9. Curing:

Allow the resin to cure according to the manufacturer's instructions. This typically involves letting it sit undisturbed for a specific period to harden.

10. Display or Use:

Your resin art piece with vinyl inserts or stickers is now ready to be displayed or used as desired! If adding more layers or color behind the add-in, you can go ahead and pour those layers now.

Whether it's a wall hanging, a coaster, or a decorative item, your creation is sure to stand out with its unique design elements.

These are some examples of finished resin pieces using vinyl inserts.

Adding Small Objects

Creating art with resin can be enhanced through the addition of various objects. A broad array of items can be incorporated into the artwork, resulting in visually appealing and one-of-a-kind pieces. Adding small trinkets or other objects can give an extra flair to your work. Here are some examples of objects you can consider incorporating:

1. Dried Flowers and Leaves: Pressed or dried flowers and leaves can add a natural and delicate touch to resin art.

Here a resin artist sprinkles glitter over her resin project.

2. Glitter and Sequins: These can add sparkle and shine to your artwork, creating a glamorous and eye-catching effect.

3. Beads and Charms: Small beads and charms can be embedded to create texture and dimension.

4. Small Shells: Shells can give a beachy and coastal vibe to your resin artwork.

5. Buttons and Jewelry: Old buttons, broken jewelry pieces, or small trinkets can be repurposed as embellishments.

6. Feathers: Feathers can add a whimsical and ethereal element to your art.

7. Confetti or Paper: Tiny pieces of colorful paper or confetti can create a playful and vibrant look.

Tip #87: For a unique twist, you can incorporate small plastic insects, toy figurines, or miniature objects.

8. Photos or Images: Tiny photographs or printed images can be sealed in resin to create a nostalgic or personalized touch.

9. Metallic Foil: Thin metallic foils can be used to create shiny accents within the resin.

This is an example of what metallic foils for resin work can look like.

10. Crystals or Gemstones: Small crystals or gemstone chips can add a touch of elegance and spirituality.

11. Wood Slices: Tiny wood slices or chips can bring a rustic and natural feel to your artwork. Just make sure the wood is sealed to avoid creating unneeded air bubbles.

12. Bits of Fabric: Small fabric scraps or ribbons can add texture and color.

13. Candy or Food Items: Edible items like sprinkles or small candies can be embedded, but be cautious of potential long-term effects.

14. Circuitry Components: For a futuristic look, you could incorporate small electronic components like resistors or LED lights.

The possibilities are nearly endless! The objects you choose should reflect your personal style and the theme or concept you have in mind for your resin artwork. Just make sure that the objects are clean, dry, and compatible with the resin and mold you are using.

Certain resin projects often incorporate personal, nostalgic items like pictures or trinkets. For instance, conducting a deep pour with silicone molds to build solid blocks of resin that include an image of their pet, a collar, and a tag is quite popular. The result is a smooth, lustrous, long-lasting memory of their pup. Here are a few things to consider when incorporating small objects into resin art:

1. Selection of Objects: Choose objects that are relatively small, lightweight, and flat.

These could include dried flowers, leaves, glitter, beads, small shells, buttons, charms, or even tiny photographs.

Tip #88: Make sure the objects are clean and dry before embedding them.

2. Preparation: Arrange your chosen objects on the surface where you plan to pour the resin. You can experiment with different layouts to find the most appealing arrangement.

3. Fixing Objects: If the objects are lightweight, they may float or move around when you pour the resin.

Tip #89: To prevent this, you can adhere them to the surface using a tiny drop of uncured resin. This will keep them in place during the pouring and curing process.

4. Layering: You can create depth and dimension by pouring resin in layers. Embed a few objects in the first layer, let it partially cure, and then add more objects in subsequent layers if you wish. This creates a visually interesting effect.

5. Positioning: Think about how the objects will be viewed from different angles. Some objects might look best when they are partially submerged in resin, while others might be better suited for placement on the surface.

6. Spacing: Be mindful of the spacing between objects. You don't want them to be too crowded, but you also want to avoid large empty spaces.

7. Encapsulation: Objects can be fully encased in resin for a smooth, glass-like finish. Alternatively, you can partially embed them, leaving some parts exposed for a more textured look.

8. Adding Color: You can tint your resin with transparent dyes or pigments to match or contrast with the colors of your objects. This can enhance the overall aesthetic of the piece.

Remember that experimentation is key to achieving the desired effect. Adding small objects to resin art allows for a lot of creative freedom and can result in stunning and unique pieces.

Chapter Summary

This section explores the fascinating realm of utilizing add-ins when it comes to resin art. It extensively explores the creative possibilities of incorporating various elements like dried flowers, vinyl inserts, and other small objects into resin creations. The chapter provides detailed guidelines on how to properly embed these add-ins, ensuring they are preserved beautifully within the resin. Additionally, it touches on the art of drying and pressing flowers, empowering artists to create their own unique botanical inclusions. By offering insights into preparation techniques and practical tips for successful incorporation, this chapter equips artists with the tools to infuse their resin artworks with personalized and stunning visual elements.

By reading through this chapter, you have learned about the following:

- how flowers must be completely dry before they are added to resin
- how to dry and press your own flowers and leaves
- how to use vinyl in resin creations
- which small objects can be added to resin
- the importance of layering when using add-ins

Chapter 9: Unmolding & Finished Product Care

How to Unmold

It's time to unmold! You have been patient, and now it is time for the absolute best part of resin work – unmolding. Unmolding your resin pieces is such a unique experience. To simply explain unmolding, slowly peel back the edges of your mold and peel away your resin piece. I find that I am always surprised by my work, even when it is exactly what I wanted or better. Seeing the final hardened, shiny piece and holding it in my hand seems unbelievable when I watch it come from a liquid base.

There are many different strategies for unmolding difficult resin pieces, but let's go over the truly effective methods.

Wait for Cure

Follow the curing time recommended by the resin manufacturer. Once the curing is complete, the resin should have solidified enough to release easily from the mold.

Tip #90: Gently bend or tap the mold to encourage the piece to come out.

Freezer Method

After the resin has partially cured, place the mold in the freezer for around 15-30 minutes. The cold temperature causes the resin to contract slightly, making it easier to pop out from the mold. Remove the mold from the freezer and flex it gently to release the piece.

Warm Water Bath

Fill a basin or bowl with warm water, around 100-120°F (37-49°C). Submerge the mold for a few minutes, allowing the heat to soften the resin. Carefully flex the mold to release the piece.

Silicone Mold Release Spray

Before pouring resin into the mold, apply a thin layer of silicone mold release spray. This helps create a barrier between the cured resin and the mold, making demolding smoother.

Flex the Mold

If using a flexible mold, gently press on the sides or back of the mold to push the resin piece out. This method works well for molds made of flexible materials like silicone or rubber.

Cutting the Mold

As a last resort, if a rigid mold won't release the piece, carefully cut the mold along the seam using a sharp craft knife or scissors. Be cautious not to cut the resin itself. This method is generally only used when all other options fail.

Doming (Adding a Topcoat)

"Doming" resin pieces involves adding a clear, glossy, and often slightly raised topcoat to enhance their appearance. This process is called "doming" because it creates a convex or rounded effect on the surface of the piece. Here's how you can do it:

1. Select the Right Resin: Choose a clear epoxy resin that is meant for doming or top coating. These resins are formulated to self-level and create a smooth, glossy finish. Make sure it's compatible with the type of resin you've used for the main piece.

2. Prepare the Surface: Ensure the resin piece you're doming is fully cured and free from dust or debris.

Tip #91: Lightly sand the surface to remove any imperfections.

3. Mix the Doming Resin: Follow the manufacturer's instructions to mix a small batch of the doming resin. Be precise with the mixing ratios to ensure proper curing.

4. Apply the Resin: Use a small pipette, syringe, or a fine-tipped brush to apply the doming resin to the surface of the piece. Start from the center and let the resin flow to the edges, allowing it to self-level.

Tip #92: Avoid overfilling, as the resin will naturally create a slightly raised dome.

5. Remove Bubbles: Use a heat gun or a lighter to gently pass over the surface. This helps to remove any trapped air bubbles.

Tip #93: Blow on the surface with a straw to pop the bubbles if you don't have a heat source.

6. Cure the Doming Resin: Allow the doming resin to cure according to the manufacturer's instructions. If using UV resin, this might involve placing the piece under a UV lamp or allowing it to air-cure for a specific period.

7. Final Touches: After the doming resin has fully cured, you'll have a glossy and elevated finish on your resin piece. If you notice any imperfections, you can lightly sand and polish the surface to achieve the desired look.

Keep in mind that doming resin can slightly alter the appearance of your piece, giving it a more polished and professional look. It's important to practice this technique on a less important piece first to become comfortable with the process and achieve the desired results.

Different Methods for Doming

Brush-On Method

Use a fine-tipped brush to carefully apply the doming resin onto the surface of the cured resin piece. This method allows for precise control over where the resin is applied and is great for smaller pieces.

Pipette or Syringe Method

Fill a plastic pipette or syringe with the doming resin and gently dispense it onto the piece. This method provides accurate placement and is particularly useful for intricate designs.

Pouring Method

For larger pieces, you can pour the doming resin directly onto the surface. Start with a small amount and let it flow to the edges, creating a smooth, raised dome.

Combination Method

Apply a thin layer of resin using a brush or pipette to create an initial base coat. Once this layer is partially cured (tacky but not fully hardened), apply a thicker layer using a pipette or pouring method to create the raised dome effect.

UV Lamp Method

If using a UV-curing doming resin, place the piece under a UV lamp designed for resin curing. This method can offer faster curing times and requires less patience compared to air curing.

Tip #94: Place the piece on a heating pad set to a low temperature to help the doming resin self-level and cure evenly.

Longevity of Resin

The longevity of resin depends on several factors, including the type of resin used, the quality of the materials, how well it's cared for, and the environmental conditions it's exposed to. Resin pieces should be kept away from extreme heat, direct sunlight, and high humidity, as these factors can accelerate the degradation of the resin and cause discoloration or warping. Different types of resins have varying degrees of durability.

Epoxy resins are generally known for their longevity and resistance to UV light, yellowing, and moisture. Polyester resins may be less durable and more prone to yellowing over time. Using high-quality resins, pigments, and additives can contribute to the longevity of your resin pieces. Cheap or subpar materials might not hold up well.

High-quality epoxy resins are often formulated to be UV resistant, meaning they won't yellow or degrade as quickly when exposed to sunlight. If you plan to display resin pieces in areas with direct sunlight, using UV-resistant epoxy can help extend their lifespan.

Tip #95: When not in use, store resin pieces in a cool, dry place away from direct sunlight.

It's important to note that while epoxy resins can provide long-lasting results, no material is entirely immune to wear and tear over time. Even the most durable resins will eventually show signs of aging. Still, with proper care and maintenance, you can extend the life and beauty of your resin creations.

Tip #96: Consider using display cases or shelves that shield the pieces from dust and environmental factors.

Chapter Summary

The beginning of this chapter discusses the steps necessary to successfully remove a resin piece from its mold. To ensure the item remains intact, one must have the right tools and be very careful with their movements. It goes on to describe "doming," which is a technique used to create a smooth, rounded finish on resin pieces. You were introduced to various doming techniques and how they improve the appearance and quality of the end product. The chapter then covers the longevity of epoxy resin pieces and how to protect them.

The five biggest lessons to take away from this chapter are:
1. Remove resin pieces from their molds slowly. Start by peeling the edges of the mold away from the piece.
2. If you are having trouble unmolding a piece, there are five helpful ways to get your piece unstuck without breaking your mold.
3. "Doming" refers to adding a topcoat to your finished resin piece.
4. Doming your resin art can help with the longevity of your art piece.
5. Never store epoxy resin pieces in direct sunlight for long periods of time.

Chapter 10: How to Handle Accidents

It's not uncommon to make mistakes while getting used to working with epoxy resins. But even if you run into trouble, don't worry - there's a solution for that! There are different ways of dealing with epoxy that hasn't cured and hardened yet, as well as when it has. From small spills to big mistakes, this chapter will explain the common accidents that can happen when working with epoxy resin and how to deal with them.

Tip #97: Think of all accidents as "happy accidents."

Finding the positive always helps you move forward with your art piece.

Resin on Skin

When working with resin for art projects, it's important to be cautious about getting resin on your skin. Resin can cause skin irritation and allergic reactions in some people.

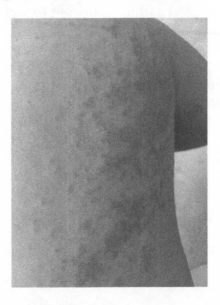

This is what a chemical rash from epoxy resin looks like.

If resin comes into contact with your skin, you should do the following:

Act Quickly

Try to wipe off the resin from your skin as soon as possible. Use a clean cloth or paper towel to gently blot and remove the resin. Avoid rubbing, as it might spread the resin further.

Tip #98: Always have alcohol wipes on hand during your crafting.

The alcohol in the wipes provides a more thorough clean if you get resin on your skin.

Wash with Soap and Water

After removing as much resin as you can, wash the area thoroughly with mild soap and water. This can help remove any remaining residue and reduce the chances of irritation.

Avoid Scratching

If you experience any itching or irritation after cleaning the area, avoid scratching it. Scratching can worsen the irritation and potentially lead to an allergic reaction.

Apply Cold Compress

If the area becomes red, itchy, or irritated, you can apply a cold compress to soothe the skin. This might help alleviate some discomfort.

Tip #99: Use a skin barrier.

Before working with resin, consider applying a barrier cream or petroleum jelly to your hands and other exposed skin areas. This can create a protective layer that makes it easier to remove resin later and minimizes direct skin contact.

Seek Medical Attention

If you experience severe skin irritation, a rash, or any unusual symptoms after contact with resin, it's best to consult a medical professional for advice and treatment.

Remember, prevention is key. Taking proper safety precautions and using protective gear can significantly reduce the risk of resin coming into contact with your skin in the first place.

If you get resin on your skin while working on resin art, several things can potentially happen. The most common reaction is skin irritation. Your skin might become red, itchy, and inflamed in the area where the resin made contact. This irritation can vary in intensity depending on the sensitivity of your skin and the duration of contact. Some people can develop allergic reactions to certain components of resin, such as the chemicals used in the resin mixture. This can lead to more severe skin symptoms, including hives, swelling, and even blisters. In extreme cases, prolonged exposure to resin on the skin can cause chemical burns. This is more likely to happen with stronger types of resin or if the resin is left on the skin for an extended period.

Repeated or prolonged exposure to resin on the skin can lead to sensitization. This means that your skin becomes increasingly sensitive to the resin's components, and even small amounts of exposure can trigger strong reactions. After my chemical reaction, I have found that even the slightest exposure leaves my skin itchy.

It's important to note that different individuals can react differently to resin exposure.

Some people might experience only mild irritation, while others could have more severe reactions. If you notice any adverse reactions after getting resin on your skin, it's best to take the necessary steps to clean the area and alleviate the symptoms. If the symptoms persist or worsen, seek medical attention. To minimize the risk, always follow safety guidelines and use protective gear when working with resin.

Resin on Surfaces

When dealing with resin for art projects, it's absolutely crucial to take necessary precautions in order to keep it from getting on unintended surfaces. Naturally, accidents do happen, and I can't possibly count how many times I have had the unfortunate problem of spilling resin on my floors or tables while I was still learning how to use resin properly. That being said, it is best to try to be as aware as possible about where the resin is going, as it can become sticky and very hard to remove once it has dried. Luckily, there are a few different strategies for removing hardened resin that one can employ when faced with this situation.

1. Scrape Off Excess Resin

If the resin is still soft or tacky, gently use a plastic scraper, an old credit card, or even your fingernail to carefully scrape off as much of the excess resin as you can.

Tip #100: Work slowly and avoid using excessive force.

You don't want to scratch or damage the surface underneath.

Tip #101: Hardened resin will often easily pop off hard surfaces (floors, tables) with ease.

Use put your scrapper under one edge and angle it up. The hardened resin should pop right off.

2. Use Heat

Apply heat to the resin to soften it. You can use a heat gun, hair dryer, or even a warm, damp cloth. Hold the heat source a few inches away from the resin and move it around to evenly distribute the heat. The goal is to soften the resin without causing any damage.

Once the resin becomes pliable, use a plastic scraper or your fingernail to gently lift and remove the softened resin.

3. Solvent Removal

Acetone is a common solvent used to remove resin. However, it can be harsh and damaging to some surfaces, such as certain plastics and painted finishes. Always test in an inconspicuous area first. Apply a small amount of acetone to a cloth or cotton ball and gently rub the resin until it starts to dissolve. Wipe away the softened resin with a clean cloth.

Tip #102: For more sensitive surfaces, consider using isopropyl alcohol instead of acetone.

4. Isopropyl Alcohol

Isopropyl alcohol can be milder than acetone and is less likely to damage surfaces. Soak a cloth or paper towel in isopropyl alcohol and gently rub the resin. The alcohol can help break down the resin and make it easier to remove. Rinse the area with water afterward to remove any alcohol residue.

5. Commercial Resin Removers

There are products specifically formulated to remove cured resin. These products are available in hardware stores and online. Follow the instructions provided on the product's packaging. Typically, you'll apply the remover, allow it to work for a specified time, and then wipe away the softened resin.

6. Mechanical Removal

In cases where the resin is very stubborn, you might need to use a combination of scraping, heat, and solvent methods. Apply the methods gently and gradually. Don't rush, as rushing can increase the risk of damaging the surface.

Remember to prioritize safety throughout the resin removal process. Use proper ventilation if you're using solvents. If you're dealing with a valuable or delicate surface, consider seeking professional help to ensure the resin is removed without causing any damage.

Flash Curing

Flash curing is a phenomenon that can occur unexpectedly during resin art projects. Specifically, it is when the resin begins to harden prematurely due to heat, light, or other chemical reactions. This results in unexpected changes in the resin's texture, coloration, and usability. It has happened to me while mixing resin in addition to pouring it into a mold. The signs of flash curing are usually visible— it often looks like the resin is rising and bloating up like a marshmallow in a microwave oven. There are numerous causes behind flash curing. High temperatures or excessive sunlight will make resin heat up faster than normal and start curing. If the molds or cups used for mixing have too much space, this can also trigger premature solidification. All in all, too much heat will cause your resin to flash cure.

Flash curing while working with epoxy resin can quickly lead to undesirable results, including shortened working time, inconsistent results, difficulty blending, and bubbling. When portions of the resin begin to cure prematurely, it limits the amount of time you have to work with it before it becomes too thick to manipulate. This can lead to uneven textures, surfaces, or color distribution, as well as visible lines or uneven transitions in different colors or layers of resin. Furthermore, flash curing can trap air bubbles within the resin, which detracts from the overall appearance of the finished piece.

In order to prevent flash curing, one must be ever vigilant. Ensure that you are working in a temperature and humidity-regulated environment; direct sunlight should be avoided at all costs. When mixing and working with resin, it is best to do so in small batches - this will reduce the amount of heat generated during the curing process.

Before starting any project, proper planning and forethought should be put into motion to ensure the material can be manipulated efficiently without sacrificing its structural integrity. In some cases, using resins with longer open times may provide more flexibility; chill pads or cool packs can also be utilized if necessary, particularly in warmer environments where flash curing is more likely to occur.

Responding to undesirable flash curing in resin art requires quick thinking and adaptability to salvage your project. Here's a step-by-step guide on how to respond effectively:

1. Stay Calm: Accidental flash curing can be frustrating, but staying calm will help you make better decisions to salvage your project.

2. Assess the Situation: Take a moment to assess how much of the resin has started to cure and where the issue is most prominent.

3. Adjust Your Approach: If only a small portion has started to cure, you might be able to work around it by adjusting your design or incorporating it into your piece.

Tip #103: If a significant portion has cured, consider adapting your design to incorporate the cured areas creatively.

4. Stop Manipulating: If you notice flash curing occurring, stop manipulating the resin in that area. Further manipulation can exacerbate the issue and affect the overall look of your artwork.

5. Use Clear or Top Layers: If a lower layer of resin has started to cure prematurely, you can often apply a clear or top layer of resin over it after it has finished curing to hide the uneven texture.

6. Create Texture: If the flash-cured areas have a different texture, consider using tools or techniques that can create a deliberate texture across your entire piece. This way, the variation won't stand out as much.

7. Blend and Distort: Incorporate techniques that intentionally blend or distort colors, such as resin manipulation, adding alcohol inks, or using other pigments to create a unique effect that complements the unintended curing.

8. Incorporate Accidents: Embrace the unexpected and view the flash curing as an opportunity to create something unique. Sometimes accidents lead to artistic discoveries.

9. Embrace Imperfection: Remember that resin art is known for its fluid and unpredictable nature. Embracing imperfections can add character to your work.

After salvaging or completing your piece, take some time to reflect on what caused the flash curing. This will help you avoid similar issues in the future. As you gain experience, you'll become more adept at preventing and responding to flash curing.

Tip #104: Continuously test new techniques and adapt your approach based on your learnings.

Every artist encounters challenges like flash curing at some point. Responding creatively and finding innovative ways to incorporate these challenges into your work can lead to unexpected and exciting outcomes. Don't be afraid to experiment and explore new techniques to transform what might seem like a setback into an opportunity for artistic growth.

Chapter Summary

This chapter opens by highlighting the artistic potential of resin but also acknowledges that many accidents can occur when dealing with the medium. The first section focuses on the inadvertent contact of resin with skin, offering insights into how to handle such accidents promptly and effectively. You learned about preventive measures, quick response techniques, and the importance of proper safety equipment to mitigate any potential harm. The second section addresses the issue of resin spillage on various surfaces. Through real-life anecdotes and practical advice, you gained a deeper understanding of how to clean and remove resin from different materials, ensuring minimal damage to their workspaces and surroundings. The chapter concludes by delving into the concept of flash curing, where resin hardens unexpectedly due to factors like heat or UV exposure. You learned how to prevent flash curing and how to salvage their projects in case it occurs, emphasizing the significance of being attentive and proactive during the resin crafting process.

After finishing reading this chapter, one should feel confident:

- when they accidentally spill resin while creating
- if resin accidentally gets on their skin
- if resin is accidentally spilled on the floor
- removing spilled liquid form and/or hardened resin
- if flash curing occurs

Resources

There are several great resources available for learning resin art, whether you're a beginner looking to get started or an experienced artist aiming to improve your skills.

Here are some of the best resources:

Online Tutorials and Courses

YouTube - Many artists and creators share detailed tutorials and demonstrations of resin art techniques on YouTube.

Skillshare - Offers a variety of online classes on resin art taught by experienced artists.

Udemy - Provides a range of resin art courses suitable for different skill levels.

Books and eBooks

Look for books dedicated to resin art techniques, tips, and project ideas. Some popular options include "Resin Jewelry" by Heidi Boyd and "The Art of Resin Jewelry" by Sherri Haab.

Online Forums and Communities

Participate in online resin art communities and forums like Reddit/ResinCasting or various Facebook groups. You can ask questions, share your work, and learn from others' experiences.

Blogs and Websites

There are numerous blogs and websites dedicated to resin art. These platforms often feature step-by-step tutorials, tips, and inspiration.

Instagram and Social Media

Follow resin artists on platforms like Instagram to see their work, techniques, and process videos. This can provide you with a lot of visual inspiration.

Craft Stores and Workshops

Some craft stores offer workshops and classes on resin art techniques. Check with local art supply shops or craft centers to see if they have any upcoming events.

Resin Manufacturers' Websites

Manufacturers often provide detailed instructions, FAQs, and tips for using their specific resin products. This can be valuable information for beginners.

Podcasts and Interviews

Some podcasts feature interviews with resin artists and experts, where they discuss techniques, experiences, and advice for aspiring resin artists.

Online Art Communities

Platforms like "Facebook" or "Reddit" have resin art pieces shared by artists, allowing you to explore different styles and techniques.

Trial and Error

Experimentation is key to learning resin art. Don't be afraid to try new techniques, mix colors, and see what works best for your style.

Frequently Asked Questions

What is resin art?

Resin art involves using a two-part epoxy resin mixture to create stunning, glossy, and durable artwork. This medium allows for various techniques, resulting in unique visual effects. One of the unique features of resin art is the way the resin self-levels and creates a smooth, glass-like surface. This makes it an ideal medium for creating pieces that resemble flowing water, glass, or other smooth surfaces.

How do I mix resin and hardener?

Resin and hardeners must be blended in the right quantity for optimal curing. Usually, a 1:1 ratio is used, but this may differ depending on the product. Accurately measure the components with labeled mixing cups and blend them slowly to avoid bubbles. Pour the hardener into the resin and mix slowly using circular strokes and figure eights to ensure that you are blending properly. Make sure to scrape the sides of the cup as needed. Mixing usually takes several minutes.

What surfaces can I apply resin to?

Resin can be applied to a wide range of surfaces, including wood, canvas, glass, acrylic, ceramic, and even fabric. The surface should be clean, dry, and free from dust to ensure proper adhesion.

How long does it take for resin to cure?

Resin typically takes about 24 to 72 hours to fully cure, depending on factors like the type of resin, temperature, and humidity.

However, it's best to wait at least 72 hours before handling the piece to ensure it's fully hardened.

What is the best way to clean resin off tools and surfaces?

Clean tools and surfaces immediately after use with rubbing alcohol or acetone to remove uncured resin. For hardened resin, gently scrape off excess material and then clean with warm soapy water.

If you want to clean any silicone materials, the best method is to submerge them in a soapy bath, let them soak, and then use gloved hands to wipe away any excess residue.

How do I create cells or lacing effects in resin?

To create cells, you can use techniques like adding silicone oil, using a heat gun or blowing air with a straw onto the resin. You can mix silicone oil into the resin before pouring it onto your surface. The silicone oil will form large cell-like bubbles as it rises through the resin mixture, creating an interesting visual effect. However, using silicone oil can be difficult to control, so use caution when adding it to your resin mixture.

Another way to create cells is by using a heat gun. When you apply heat to the surface of the resin, air bubbles are created, which form beautiful patterns. Keep in mind that this technique can be unpredictable, so practice on a piece of scrap material first before applying it to your artwork.

For lacing effects, gently drag a tool through the resin to create intricate patterns. You can also use a straw or other tool to blow air onto the surface of the resin while it is curing for an interesting lacing effect. Start by lightly blowing across the surface and then experiment with different techniques until you achieve your desired look.

How do I deal with resin that's not setting or curing properly?

If you're dealing with resin that isn't setting properly, there could be a few reasons behind it. Resin requires precise mixing of its components, usually resin and hardener.

Ensure you are using the correct ratio as specified by the manufacturer. Even a small deviation can affect the curing process.

Inadequate mixing can lead to improper curing. Make sure to mix the resin and hardener thoroughly, scraping the sides and bottom of the container to incorporate all parts.

Both temperature and humidity can influence resin curing. If the environment is too cold or too humid, it can slow down the curing process. Check the recommended temperature range provided by the manufacturer and consider using a space heater or dehumidifier if needed.

Resin has a limited shelf life. Using old or expired resin can result in incomplete curing.

Make sure you're using fresh materials.

Altitude can affect the curing time of resin. If you're at a high altitude, you might need to adjust your curing times accordingly.

If you're adding pigments, dyes, or other additives to the resin, under-mixing or over-mixing can affect curing.

If you've considered these factors and your resin still isn't setting properly, it's a good idea to reach out to the manufacturer for specific guidance or consider consulting experienced resin artists for advice.

How do I create resin geode art?

To create resin geode art, start with a slab of clear or translucent resin and add layers of colored resin to form swirling patterns that mimic the look of cut gems. To make them look like you found them in nature, use techniques like pouring clear resin on top of colored layers and pulling the resin slowly through an old butter knife or spatula to make marbled patterns.

How do I avoid resin yellowing over time?

To avoid resin yellowing over time, use high-quality, UV-resistant resins. Keep finished pieces away from direct sunlight, and consider applying a UV-resistant varnish or sealant to protect against yellowing. Store your resin in shaded, cool areas.

Can I paint over the top of cured resin?

Yes, you can paint on resin that has completely hardened. First, sand the surface lightly so that the paint adheres better. Wipe off any dust and clean it thoroughly with denatured alcohol or a solvent-based cleaner. Then apply acrylic paints or other compatible mediums.

How do I store leftover resin?

Store unused resin components in their original containers, sealed tightly. Keep them in a cool, dry place away from direct sunlight. Avoid mixing larger batches than needed to minimize waste. Once the hardener has been added to the resin, any extra mixed resin will no longer be salvageable if unused.

Can I use any type of pigment with resin?

Not all pigments are compatible with resin. It's best to use pigments specifically formulated for resin art. These can include liquid pigments, powders, and even alcohol inks. Always do a small test before using a new pigment.

How do I prevent bubbles in resin?

Bubbles are common in resin art. You can reduce them by mixing the resin slowly, using a heat gun or torch to pop bubbles, and pouring resin in thin layers. Warm your resin before mixing to decrease viscosity and minimize air entrapment.

Can I use epoxy resin on canvas?

Yes, you can apply resin to canvas. However, you'll need to create a barrier to prevent the resin from leaking through. This can be achieved by taping the back of the canvas or applying a layer of gesso.

Can I use resin to cover acrylic paintings?

Yes, you can apply resin over acrylic paintings to protect and enhance them. Ensure the acrylic paint is fully dried and free from any moisture or oils before applying the resin.

How do I achieve a glossy finish with resin?

To get a glossy finish, make sure your surface is level before pouring a doming layer of resin. Pour in thin layers to avoid excessive heat buildup, which can lead to a cloudy finish. Use a heat gun to remove bubbles and achieve a smooth, glossy surface.

To achieve a glossy finish without doming, use a shiny silicone mold. The shine from the mold will transfer to your finished resin piece.

Can I add objects like dried flowers or shells into resin?

Yes, you can embed various objects into resin to create unique effects. Make sure the objects are dry and free from moisture to prevent cloudiness in the resin. Arrange them in the resin and pour in layers to prevent sinking.

What safety precautions should I take when working with resin?

Safety is crucial. Work in a well-ventilated area or wear a respirator. Wear gloves and protective clothing to avoid skin contact. Avoid inhaling fumes. Read and follow the manufacturer's safety guidelines.

How do I price and sell resin artworks?

Pricing depends on factors like size, complexity, materials used, and your experience.

Research similar artworks, consider how much it will cost you to make your artwork, and factor in how long it takes you to finish a piece. Selling platforms like Etsy or local art shows can be great places to start.

What is the difference between epoxy resin and polyester resin?

Epoxy resin is generally more popular for art due to its clarity, UV resistance, and low toxicity. Polyester resin is less commonly used and can be more brittle. Epoxy resin also cures more slowly, allowing for intricate designs.

About the Author

Madison Barclay, a skilled artist, and creative enthusiast, brings a wealth of passion and expertise to the world of resin art. With over three years of dedicated experience in the field, Madison's artistic journey has been marked by innovation and a commitment to pushing the boundaries of resin artistry.

At the age of 26, Madison's artistic prowess shines through as she manages two thriving Etsy shops, each reflecting their distinct creative flair. ArtsyFartsyMaddi showcases Madison's mastery of resin, while iArtsyFartsyMaddi offers a collection of captivating digital products.

Madison's Instagram, "artsyfartsymaddi," serves as a captivating window into her artistic universe, offering a glimpse into the captivating world of resin creations that come to life under her expert touch. Beyond her flourishing artistic pursuits, Madison's engagement in the literary realm as a burgeoning author in both non-fiction and fiction genres adds another layer to her creative journey. With experience as a ghostwriter, Madison's storytelling ability resonates through her words.

Happily married and accompanied by an eight-month-old golden retriever, Madison finds inspiration in the tapestry of life's experiences and the nature around her, shaping her artistry and enriching her creative expression.

HowExpert publishes how to guides on all topics from A to Z by everyday experts. Visit HowExpert.com to learn more.

About the Publisher

Byungjoon "BJ" Min / 민병준 is a Korean American author, publisher, entrepreneur, and founder of HowExpert. He started off as a once broke convenience store clerk to eventually becoming a fulltime internet marketer and finding his niche in publishing. The mission of HowExpert is to discover, empower, and maximize everyday people's talents to ultimately make a positive impact in the world for all topics from A to Z. Visit BJMin.com and HowExpert.com to learn more. John 14:6

Recommended Resources

- HowExpert.com – How To Guides on All Topics from A to Z by Everyday Experts.
- HowExpert.com/free – Free HowExpert Email Newsletter.
- HowExpert.com/books – HowExpert Books
- HowExpert.com/courses – HowExpert Courses
- HowExpert.com/clothing – HowExpert Clothing
- HowExpert.com/membership – HowExpert Membership Site
- HowExpert.com/affiliates – HowExpert Affiliate Program
- HowExpert.com/jobs – HowExpert Jobs
- HowExpert.com/writers – Write About Your #1 Passion/Knowledge/Expertise & Become a HowExpert Author.
- HowExpert.com/resources – Additional HowExpert Recommended Resources
- YouTube.com/HowExpert – Subscribe to HowExpert YouTube.
- Instagram.com/HowExpert – Follow HowExpert on Instagram.
- Facebook.com/HowExpert – Follow HowExpert on Facebook.
- TikTok.com/@HowExpert – Follow HowExpert on TikTok.